$4.00
oversize

The Real Love

THE COMPLETE BOOK, LYRICS AND SHEET MUSIC OF THE MUSICAL

Inspired by a true story

Foreword by
Richard Maltby, Jr.

Introduction by
Al Kasha

Lyrics based on poems by
Supreme Master Ching Hai

Music by
Bill Conti • Al Kasha • Doug Katsaros • Don Pippin • David Shire

Book by
Frank Evans & Tom Shelton

Art Director: Peter Peace
Design: Sondra Yard, Sam Bobb
Editor: Toni Greene
Copy Editors: Sara Kudinsky, Lisa Parker
Photographs: Ross Bird, Steve Cohn, Robert Millard, Scott Young
Color Management: Wang Bor Tang, Yu Hui-Chun

ISBN 978-986-6895-61-6

First edition: August 2012
Second edition: October 2012
10 9 8 7 6 5 4 3 2

Publisher: The Supreme Master Ching Hai International Association Publishing Co., Ltd.
No. 236 Songshan Road, Taipei, Formosa (Taiwan), R.O.C.
www.smchbooks.com
E-mail: smchbooks@Godsdirectcontact.org
Tel: +886-2-87873935
Fax: +886-2-87870873

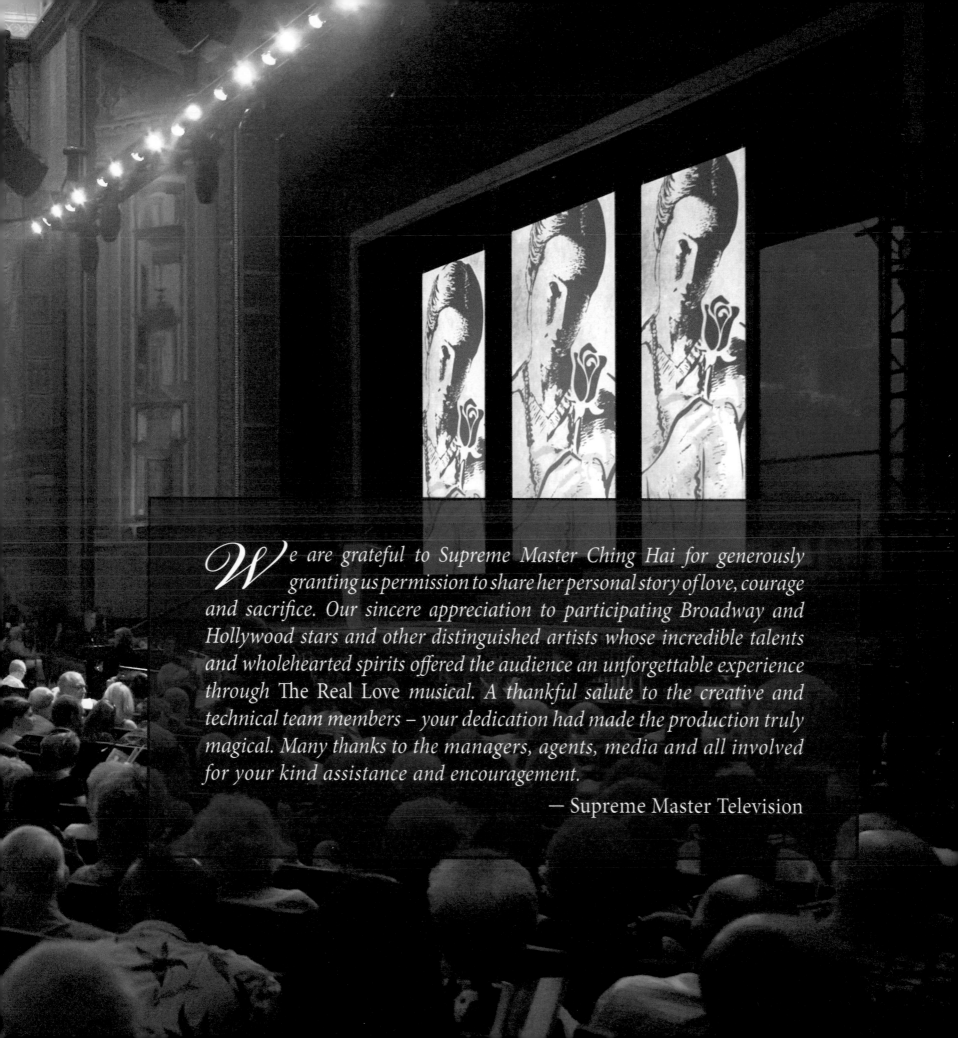

*W*e are grateful to Supreme Master Ching Hai for generously granting us permission to share her personal story of love, courage and sacrifice. Our sincere appreciation to participating Broadway and Hollywood stars and other distinguished artists whose incredible talents and wholehearted spirits offered the audience an unforgettable experience through The Real Love musical. A thankful salute to the creative and technical team members – your dedication had made the production truly magical. Many thanks to the managers, agents, media and all involved for your kind assistance and encouragement.

— Supreme Master Television

CONTENTS

FOREWORD

Supreme Master Ching Hai's journey is a story of love and spiritual discovery, and what better way to bring such a story to life than through music – that is to say, by telling the story in the form of a musical.

The great contribution of the United States to theatrical tradition is the invention of the American musical. Over the past 100 years, American artists have combined elements of opera, operetta, popular songwriting, jazz, vaudeville, etc. into a unique art form. And over the past 50 years, songwriters and playwrights have pushed that form into new and exciting expressions. The dramatic possibilities of storytelling through music, songs, dance, and musical playwriting have been explored with ever-increasing daring and invention – leading to great musicals such as *West Side Story, My Fair Lady*, and *Fiddler on the Roof* – the list is endless. More recently, European artists such as Andrew Lloyd Webber (*The Phantom of the Opera, Cats*) and Alain Boublil and Claude-Michel Schönberg (*Les Misérables, Miss Saigon*) have added additional opera grandeur to the mix.

What these artists have done in the creation of the modern musical is to explore the power of song to touch human hearts. If a story is about love or

a spiritual topic, or both, only music can truly take the audience on a journey into the realm where these passions come alive and are viscerally felt.

The Real Love is based on the Supreme Master's personal life experiences. It tells the story of a young Vietnamese woman (Thanh) living in Munich, deeply involved with the plight of the refugees. A romantic poet at heart, she falls in love with a handsome German doctor (Rolf) and they marry, but an uneasiness grows in her heart. Her work with refugees expands into a concern for all humankind, and it becomes clear to her that she is destined to pursue a spiritual quest in her life – one that must involve traveling to India, far away from her beloved husband, for an indefinite time. Her husband, a man of science whose medical training has led him to trust in facts, not spiritual ephemera, finds Thanh's choice too lofty, but he loves her and wants her to do what will bring her happiness. Thanh asks Rolf to come with her, but he is reluctant to abandon his medical practice, and so Thanh must go on her journey alone. Their devotion to each other never wanes, and Rolf even goes to India to find Thanh. But by now Thanh has realized more clearly than ever that their journeys are meant to be

different, and hers is one that must take her – alone – into the sacred Himalayan mountains where she hopes to meet an enlightened Master and attain the key to everlasting happiness and inner peace. Rolf and Thanh part, but their love does not die.

This, as one can see, is a story that takes place in the human heart. It is a battle of conflicting loves, a conflict between human connection and spiritual devotion. The challenge in telling such a story is: how to make people feel the passions that live inside the narrative. The answer, of course, is to use music. Thomas Clinton, in his 1983 book, *Music as Heard*, says, "Music is not a fact or a thing – but a meaning constituted by human beings." Music is the gateway to the soul, a means of defining and making tangible feelings and sensations that cannot otherwise be expressed. So to tell a love story that is also the story of a young woman's journey into the spirit, music has to be employed.

Once the decision was made to tell this great love story as a musical, it became a question not of what, but who. Some of the most talented artists in America were enlisted to bring Supreme Master Ching Hai's story to life. Multi-award-winning

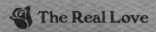

writers (Frank Evans and Tom Shelton) contributed the script; five of Broadway and Hollywood's most distinguished and honored composers (Bill Conti, Al Kasha, Doug Katsaros, Don Pippin, David Shire) agreed to contribute the music. As for the lyrics, it was not necessary to comb the world for a brilliant, talented artist. The source for the lyrics was right at home.

All her life, Supreme Master Ching Hai has written poetry. She conveyed the feelings that passed through her heart and mind as she lived her life in powerfully rich verses, in imagistic writing that turned human events into poetic expression. These poems have been collected into a number of books (*Silent Tears*, *The Dream of a Butterfly*, *Wu Tzu Poems*, *Traces of Previous Lives*, *The Love of Centuries*, to name just a few) that defined her journey as eloquently and lyrically as any Broadway musical. And so the obvious decision was made to use some of these poems as the lyrics for the songs in the musical. The composers had freedom to adapt the verses as they saw fit. Often they set the poems intact; in other cases, they reorganized the content of the poem to fit a more standard song form. But the words in the songs are all those of Supreme Master Ching Hai.

Finally, a group of exceptional actors was assembled to bring the story to human life on the stage, along with the kind of gigantic support team of director, choreographers, designers, and technicians that any modern musical requires. Led by outstanding stars such as award-winning Joanna Ampil, Tony winners Daisy Eagan and Cady Huffman, and Tony nominees Adam Pascal and Robert Torti, the cast made these real-life people stage characters — memorable, funny, and thrillingly touching.

Any musical is the result of a multitude of talented artists working together. Creating a musical is almost a metaphor for the message that Supreme Master Ching Hai shares: that people must come together in love. What is a musical actually but a variety of disparate people coming together to lavish their love and knowledge upon the joint creation of a single work of art, a work of art that is in itself the very embodiment of love?

In a very real sense, this musical, *The Real Love*, is a continuation of the spiritual message the Supreme Master spreads to the world. Events in her own life take on a spiritual journey we can all relate to — one that leads us deeper and deeper into the mysteries and wonders of the human heart and the human soul. In creating this musical, the artists have taken the journey with Supreme Master Ching Hai, and now that it is a complete work of art, it is here for you to experience as well.

— Richard Maltby, Jr.
Tony & Olivier Award-winning director
(Ain't Misbehavin', Fosse) & lyricist *(Miss Saigon)*

Supreme Master Ching Hai
Early 1980s
Photo courtesy of Dr. Dr. Rolf G.

INTRODUCTION

"Supreme Master Ching Hai perfectly demonstrates our potential to be both fully human and fully divine…"

When looking for a story to tell through music, one premise that I always search for is an interesting clash between two separate worlds that, through love, finally come together. Supreme Master Ching Hai's life is ripe for this kind of storytelling. Supreme Master, who was born in Vietnam, and her love interest Rolf, being from a different background, offer the foundation of an inspiring story, and one that can be readily told in the theatrical medium. Her choice to sacrifice her own love and contentment for the service of the multitude, though difficult, is one to be applauded as her own happiness plays second fiddle to the joy that she has since created in the world.

Supreme Master Ching Hai perfectly demonstrates our potential to be both fully human and fully divine, shining as an example to those of us striving for the same balance. One place where this is truly apparent is in her poetry. While reviewing the poems that Supreme Master composed, I was touched by her commitment to bring the world to an inner peace and received the inspiration to create a musical about her life story based on her profound verses. Each of the poems Supreme Master composed dealt with both the physical and the spiritual of how to consume nourishment through her choice of foods and prayer. Through her poetic nature the human qualities and divinity

that she strives for were pulled together and conveyed in her poems. Adding music gave a further, richer dimension for this work to be turned into a musical.

It has truly been an honor to collaborate on this musical as we come to rejoice in the melding of two worlds and to make this Earth a better place to live, to work and to survive together for a peaceful future.

—Al Kasha
Two-time Academy Award winner
(The Poseidon Adventure, Seven Brides for Seven Brothers)

CAST & CREDITS

Broadcast live globally for Supreme Master Television's 5th Anniversary, the world premiere of *The Real Love* musical was presented in front of a full house at The Pasadena Civic Auditorium, California, USA on August 27, 2011 with the following cast:

THE REAL LOVE: FEATURE SONG

POEM by Supreme Master Ching Hai
MUSIC by Don Pippin

GUEST STARS
Betty Buckley
Filippa Giordano
Shirley Jones
Trent Kowalik
Kiril Kulish
Faith Rivera
Tom Schmid
Lynne Winterstelter

DIRECTOR
Cheryl Baxter

MUSICAL DIRECTOR
Scott Lavender

STAGE MANAGER
David Lober

THE REAL LOVE: THE MUSICAL

Lyrics based on poems by
Supreme Master Ching Hai

Music by
Bill Conti, Al Kasha,
Doug Katsaros,
Don Pippin, David Shire

Book by
Frank Evans and Tom Shelton

CAST
Joanna Ampil *(Thanh)*
Glory Curda *(Linh)*
Daisy Eagan *(Greta)*
Cady Huffman *(Elsa)*
Mueen Jahan *(Rajeev/Sadhu)*
Shirley Jones *(Mother-in-Law)*
Adam Pascal *(Rolf)*
Robert Torti *(Klaus)*
Dick Van Patten *(Father-in-Law)*

ENSEMBLE
Ryan Castellino
Laura Castle
Jay Donnell
Clémence du Barré
Clayton Farris
Zachary Ford
Stephanie Hayslip
LaTonya Holmes
Rebecca Ann Johnson
Michael J. Marchak
Carlos Martin
Bruce Merkle
Marc Oka
Domonique Paton
Michiko Sasaki
Alonzo Saunders
Leah Seminario

David Raimo
Nikki Tomlinson
Karen Volpe
Erin Zaruba

Producers
Peter Peace, Paula Holt,
Doug Katsaros

Associate Producer
Tom Ware

Director
Chris Shelton

Choreographer
Mark Knowles

Set Designer
Gary Wissman

Costume Designer
Kate Bergh

Lighting Designer
Darryl Palagi

Orchestrations
Doug Katsaros

Musical Director
David O

Stage Manager
Hethyr (Red) Verhoef

Casting Director
Michael Donovan, CSA

Associate Casting Director
Peter Matyas, CSA

Set Design Assistant
Michael Field

Projection Designer
Jason Thompson

Assistant Projection Designer
Kaitlyn Pietras

Sound Designer
Cricket S. Myers

Property Master
Kirk Graves

Acting Coach
Tracy Winters

Wig & Hair Designer
Rick Geyer

Wig Assistants
Judy Blanchard, Rose Marie
Ranallo

Hairstylists
Ann Fan, Daphne Tie, Carolyn
Trane, Manny Wynn

Makeup Artists
Frida DeOrellana, Iris Headman,
Mimi Park, Sherilyn Stetz, Hương Vũ

Assistant Costume Designer
Michelle Neumann

Assistant Costumer
Rhea Bothe

Wardrobe Dressers
Tanya Apuya, Timo Elliott,
Hannah Greene, Cindy Hong,
Turk Magnanti, Minta Manning,
Elyse Taylor, Elizabeth Teemley

Seamstress
Trish Keen, Tilda Lee

Assistant to Director
Aylia Colwell

Assistant Stage Manager
Jessica Aguilar

Production Assistants
Jon Eidson, Michael Field

Photographers
Ross Bird, Steve Cohn, Robert
Millard, Scott Young

ORCHESTRA

Conductor
David O

WINDS
Reed 1-Flute, Clarinet, Wood Flute
Carol Chaikin
Reed 2-Clarinet, Bass Clarinet
Brian Walsh
Reed 3-Oboe, English Horn
Maya Barrera

BRASS
French Horns
Amy Sanchez, Allen Fogle
Trumpet, Flugelhorn
Erick Jovel
Trombone, Bass Trombone
Denis Jiron

RHYTHM
Timpani and Percussion
Joey Muskat
Drum Kit, Octopad
Kurt Walther
Electric and Acoustic Guitar
John Storie
Keyboards
Brian Kennedy

STRINGS
Violins
Steve Huber, Paul Cartwright, Yvette
Holzwarth, Ina Veli, Alwyn Wright
Violas
Tom Lea, Mike Whitson
Cello
John Krovoza
Acoustic and Electric Bass
Mark Breitenbach

VIDEO PRODUCTION
Production Manager
Keith Dixon
Production Coordinator
Laurie Wright
Video Director
Mark Mardoyan
Technical Director
Chris Savage
Script Supervisor / Assistant Director
Stephanie Rondeau
Assistant Director
Steve Blum
Video Control
Keith Anderson, Peter Standel
Videotape Operator
Steve Benlien
Camera Operators
Ray Dominguez, Mac McIntyre,
Kevin Michele, Jamie Morris, Phil
Solomon, Chris Tallen
Dolly Operator
Mark Putnum
Steadicam Operator
Steve Field
Jib Operators
Alex Hernandez, Mark Kuntz
Video Utility
Hilton Brown, Dan YEL Lopez,
John MacGregor, Dan Mardoyan
Video Project Manager
Hank Moore
Video Engineer In Charge Mobile Unit
Bryan Anderson
Video Maintenance Engineer Mobile Unit
Adam Harding
Video Utility Mobile Unit
Stephen Law Lead
Projectionist
Tari Karkanen
Video Camera Utility
Patrick "TC" Iglin
Assistant Lighting Designer
Rachel Miller
Lighting Programmer
Steve "six-pack" Hagerman
Electrician - Moving Light Technician
Eric Barth, Eric Pelaez
Audio Engineer In Charge
Trace Goodman
Audio Engineer / Front of House
Gabe Benso

Audio Engineer / Monitors
Danny Williams
Audio Engineer / Vocals, Broadcast Mobile Unit
Ramone Montoya
Audio Engineer / Music Mix / Broadcast Mobile Unit
Peter Baird
Audio Systems / Mobile Unit Technician
Tim Van Given
Audio Systems / Intercom Technician
Christian Berry
Audio Systems / Wireless Technician
Curtis Anderson
Project Manager / Power
Candace Saunders
Lead Power Technician
Rick Wheeler
FM Language Interpretation
RJ Steventon
FM Language Interpretation Engineer
Marvin Hall

LIVE BROADCAST & VIDEOCONFERENCE
Broadcast Streaming IT
Quincy Vogel, Phoebe Vuong
Conference Video Switcher
Vince Lu
Conference Audio Engineer / Digital Recording
Andy F. Chern
Conference Audio Engineer / Broadcast Mix
Theo Wynne
Projection Switcher
Lloyd Famy
Video Utility
Trevor Van

LIVE HIGH-DEFINITION VIEWING ROOM
Production Coordinator
Michael Crowell
Video Projectionist
Tari Karkanen
Audio Engineer
Jason Lloyd
Video Utility
Tim Pong

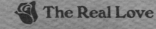

The Real Love
THE MUSICAL

THANH A lovely, petite and spiritually-oriented Vietnamese woman. Quiet and caring, she has a good sense of humor and the romantic nature of a true poet.

ROLF A handsome German doctor with kind, blue eyes and a sharp wit. A man of science who is deeply committed to his medical practice.

KLAUS The hospital's eccentric and charming dietician, with an unrequited love for Thanh.

ELSA Thanh's German friend and co-worker at the Red Cross. An attractive and materialistic but goodhearted blonde.

GRETA A talented artist with an optimistic personality, interested in Eastern mysticism and vegetarianism.

RAJEEV A down-to-earth Indian doctor who is Rolf's colleague and Greta's husband.

LINH An orphaned 8-year-old refugee girl from Vietnam.

SCENES

The Real Love
THE MUSICAL

Act One takes place in the late 1970s in Munich, Germany.

ACT ONE
SCENE 1. Red Cross office and a flashback of Vietnam
SCENE 2. The hospital
SCENE 3. A restaurant
SCENE 4. Streets of Munich
SCENE 5. Wedding reception hall
SCENE 6. The hospital
SCENE 7. Streets of Munich
SCENE 8. The hospital – Rolf's office
SCENE 9. A disco club
SCENE 10. Thanh and Rolf's home
SCENE 11. Streets of Munich
SCENE 12. The hospital
SCENE 13. Greta's studio
SCENE 14. The hospital

Act Two mainly takes place in India and the Himalayas.

ACT TWO
SCENE 1. Streets of Delhi
SCENE 2. Sadhu's temple
SCENE 3. The forest
SCENE 4. Bridge in Munich, Germany
SCENE 5. The Ganges riverbank
SCENE 6. Delhi
SCENE 7. Mud house in Rishikesh
SCENE 8. Streets of Rishikesh
SCENE 9. Mud house in Rishikesh
SCENE 10. Pathway up the Himalayas
SCENE 11. Gangotri and higher Himalayan regions

 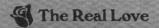

Musical Numbers

THE REAL LOVE: FEATURE SONG

Lyrics by Supreme Master Ching Hai

Music by Don Pippin

The Real Love
THE MUSICAL

ACT I

1. Overture ....Orchestra
2. What Can I Do with My Heart...Thanh
3. Yearning for Past Spring...Thanh and Vietnamese Villagers
4. You and the Kingdom .... Rolf
5. Moon of Mine ....Thanh and Rolf
6. I Believe Only in Love .... Wedding Singer
7. Since We Knew Each Other..Wedding Guests
8. I Believe Only in Love (reprise) ....Elsa
9. Weekend Thoughts ....Thanh
10. On the Riverbank Disco ....Orchestra
11. Self Confession ....Elsa
12. Search High and Low ....Greta
13. For the One Who Stayed Behind ....Thanh and Rolf

ACT II

14. Welcome to India..Indian Crowd
15. The God Seeker ....Thanh
16. P.S. Till Tomorrow ....Thanh
17. Do You Miss Me, Darling...Rolf
18. On the Riverbank...Thanh
19. If It Wasn't for Sprouts in Life ....Klaus
20. Our Time..Thanh and Rolf
21. Ganga Ma... Pilgrims
22. The Peace Seeker..Company

Lyrics based on poems by Supreme Master Ching Hai (except for No. 14 and 21), No. 5, 15, 17, 22 music by Bill Conti,
No. 3, 4, 6, 20 music by Al Kasha, No. 14, 21 music by Doug Katsaros, No. 2, 7, 9, 12, 19 music by Don Pippin,
No. 11, 13, 16 music by David Shire, No. 10, 18 music by Supreme Master Ching Hai

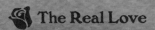

This song is like twelve songs to me because it says so much. It's overwhelming in the most beautiful sense of that word. There's just so much richness in the imagery that Supreme Master Ching Hai chooses."

FAITH RIVERA
Emmy Award-winning singer

THE REAL LOVE: FEATURE SONG

Lyrics by Supreme Master Ching Hai
Music by Don Pippin
Vocals by Guest Stars & Company

They said:
"The world is small"
But it ain't that small!
There's plenty room
For you and me and all…

So why this bickering with our neighbor
For a few meters more –
Even a few kilometers,
Or say another mountain and river!
Don't you feel rather "small"?

At the end of our sojourn
What do we get after all?
One squeezy square meter
If we are lucky!
To lie down forever

Let's share the splendid Earth
And do everything to make it better
Even the worms don't rival
With the butterflies or the birds
Why do we humans try so mightily?
Against each other
Make life a real misery
And even shorter!

What will we tell at the Buddha's gate,
Or to Saint Peter?
All the stuff we did on Earth,
To bring pain and to suffer…
Oh dear man!

Let me tell you something
Just go hang…
Yourself on the hammock
Between the shadowing coconut
Graceful tall trees!

Enjoy some cake and tea
Feel the gentle breeze
That cools all folly

There…there! You see!
…Ah!..tons of things
We can do our heart to please
Some small and great pleasure
Let it all be…
Let's make life more simple
Let our demands be little.
Then you'll know
Happiness ever more and more!

Then we don't have to go on snatching land,
Nor have we to hurry on converting man:
It's not how many in a belief system
It's what becomes of them!
It's not the name of a religious order
It's what we make of the name!
It's not how crowded a religion
It's how much into world peace their contribution
It's not our words
It's rather louder our actions.
What is going to be our legend
In the long history of humans?
Will it be right and just
Will it be noble and benevolent?
Or just a grim picture
Soaked in anguished bloody paint!

Why always boast about our Heavenly root:
Oh! Almighty God's beloved children!
While our life is tainted with all evils
While our survival
Is the cost of others' extinction!

What is the mark of the "chosen"?
Is it just the bloodstain on your hands?
Be it from animals or man's!

Oh my dear brothers
I wanted to write you a long loving letter
With thousands more questioning words
But I am dumbfounded
Watching the madness
Of it all.
Tell me:
When or will we ever
Represent Heaven on Earth?

The Real Love

Script & Lyrics

ACT ONE

SCENE ONE
MUNICH RED CROSS OFFICE

It is late 1970s in Munich, Germany. The Red Cross is helping refugees of conflicts around the world to settle into their new environs. At the Red Cross office, ELSA, the receptionist, sits at her desk painting her fingernails. The phone rings.

ELSA: Munich Red Cross, Elsa speaking. How may I direct your call? *(Recognizing the caller is a man, she immediately speaks in a low and sultry voice. Languidly fingering a stack of brochures)* Oh, I seeeee... Well, I could definitely tell you how you can get more involved with our humanitarian work, Doctor. *(Listens.)* Actually, it might be better if you just came down and picked up the literature yourself. We're at 127 Hegelstrasse – *(Listens; her voice hardens.)* Your wife is in the area? Nevermind, I'll mail 'em to you. *(Hangs up and resumes painting her nails. A RED CROSS WORKER walks in with an armful of files.)*

RED CROSS WORKER: Where's Thanh?

ELSA: Who knows?

WORKER: Well then, here – you can start on these.

ELSA: Good Lord – !?!

WORKER: New arrivals. Vietnamese, mostly.

THANH: (entering) More boat people. Dozens of them.

ELSA: All right, Bright Eyes, got any bright ideas what we're going to do with your new friends?

THANH: It is done. I have reorganized three storage rooms. Found space for three dozen bunk beds.

WORKER: (full of admiration) You're astounding! What exactly is your official job description around here?

ELSA: Interpreter! And that is it! Sometimes I think she's running for Director-General of the International Red Cross...!

THANH: (troubled by ELSA's remark; softly) No...no...that is not true. I just want to be helpful. These refugees have lost everything. If I hadn't left Vietnam to study abroad – by sheer chance and good luck – I could have been one of them. Do you see?

(A beat. Then WORKER leaves quietly.)

ELSA: (quieter; humbled a bit) Hey, do you want some tea? It's chrysanthemum. That stuff you gave me.

THANH: Yes, please, thank you. Lovely. *(She sits.)*

ELSA: So, what's next for you today?

THANH: Escorting refugees to the hospital. Picking them up in the afternoon.

ELSA: Why don't you pick me up one of those cute doctors while you're at it?

THANH: Oh! My poem! So, did he like it?

ELSA: Oh, not exactly. And by the way, you're fired.

THANH: What?

ELSA: As a ghost-writer you make an excellent vegetarian chef. Your poem was so sweet he did not believe for a minute that I could have written it. Slightly humiliated, I admitted that it was yours. Now he wants to meet YOU!

THANH: (laughing) Oh Elsa! I knew this was a bad idea from the beginning!

ELSA: No, no, no, no, I need a new one for a new prospect. A poem that sounds just like me.

THANH: Alright, let me see what I have. *(She opens her journal.)*
Here's one:

If there wasn't you in life
Where to would I have gone?
Maybe to a monastery

But there I must be so lonely
Like a nun without a monk!

ELSA: A nun? Me!?! C'mon, be serious!

THANH: Sorry, love. Try me again tomorrow. What was his name, anyway?

ELSA: Which one?

THANH: Your would-be doctor-husband-benefactor.

ELSA: Rolf Reinhardt. Chief of Epidemiology!

THANH: Aiming high!

ELSA: You know, I've got a thing for powerful men, Thanh. And the powerful Mercedes 450 SLs they tend to drive...! But I'm done with doctors – they're too busy for me. I've moved on to Heinrich, the high financier.

THANH: Elsa, you and your obsession with men…it all seems beside the point to me.

ELSA: Beside the point?! You could have any man you want, with that gorgeous face and that huge heart of yours!

THANH: Well, maybe that's just my problem.

"WHAT CAN I DO WITH MY HEART"

THANH:
WHAT CAN I DO WITH MY HEART?
THIS LITTLE HEART OF MINE
SO LITTLE AND SO FINE!
THIS LITTLE HEART OF MINE!

WHAT CAN I DO WITH MY HEART?
SHE WOULDN'T LET ME FREE
IT HURTS ME SO MUCH DAILY
WITH EVERY MISFORTUNE I SEE

WHAT CAN I DO FOR THE PEOPLE?
WHAT CAN I DO FOR THE WORLD?
ALWAYS FULL OF TROUBLES,
ALWAYS FULL OF SORROW!

WHAT CAN I DO WITH MY HEART?

THIS LITTLE HEART OF MINE
SO LITTLE AND SO FINE!
THIS LITTLE HEART OF MINE!

HERE'S WHAT I'LL DO WITH MY HEART
IF THE WORLD DOESN'T HURT
THEN MY HEART DOESN'T HURT
THAT'S WHAT I'LL DO FOR MY HEART
THAT'S WHAT I'LL DO FOR MY WORLD

ELSA: I absolutely adore you, even though you drive me absolutely crazy. You want to take care of the whole world, but you won't let someone take care of YOU...!

RED CROSS WORKER: (entering) Thanh! They're asking for you in the barracks.

THANH: (to WORKER) Thank you. *(Exiting, she blows a kiss to ELSA.)* – Tomorrow, a poem that sounds exactly like you!

(Crossfade to a hallway of the barracks. THANH encounters an AFRICAN REFUGEE on crutches.)

THANH: Wasafa! How is your leg?

AFRICAN REFUGEE: Thanks to you, SO much better! Would you like to dance? *(Hands his crutches to a friend.)*

THANH: I would love to!

(They do a brief waltz twirl. The REFUGEE stumbles.)

THANH: Oh, careful.

AFRICAN REFUGEE: Oh, yes.

THANH: Are you okay?

AFRICAN REFUGEE: Yes, sorry.

(They both laugh. THANH moves to a group of VIETNAMESE REFUGEES.)

REFUGEE #1: Thanh, this is the little girl, Linh.

THANH: (to an 8-year-old Vietnamese girl) Sweetheart. Why are you trembling, dear?

 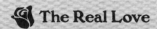

What can I do for the world?
What can I do for my people?
Always full of troubles,
Always full of sorrow!

Excerpt of "Cannot Do a Thing with My Heart"
Poem by Supreme Master Ching Hai, written in her late 20s
Munich, Germany - September 1978

LINH: *(very scared)* I have dreams. Bad ones... Nightmares.

THANH: *(embracing her impulsively)* You're safe here, sweetheart.

REFUGEE #1: Thanh, what did we do so wrong to deserve this? Is it karma?

THANH: *(struggling for an answer)* Sometimes we cannot find the reason for everything that happens.

REFUGEE #2: What will happen next?

THANH: I don't know. *(a beat)* But we're going to enroll you all in school – and you can be anything you want to be!

LINH: I want to be a teacher!

THANH: You will be a wonderful teacher. But for now, you need to rest, just rest.

REFUGEE #3: *(pulling THANH aside; sotto voce)* She was the sole survivor in her boat. Father, mother, older brother – ALL killed before her eyes.

REFUGEE #1: Pirates. Barbarians! Club and knife the men; rape the women; throw the babies overboard.

REFUGEE #2: Giant waves crashing down. One hundred forty people hurled into the sea. I hung to a splinter of wood. God knows what happened to the others.

REFUGEE #3: But you were lucky! When my cousin came out of the water – his legs were eaten off by sharks.

THANH: Oh dear God, what can I do? If there's anything I can do to help relieve their suffering, I vow to help. My dear friends! In this new place, you will find stability to re-invent your lives. And always remember that we will have the memories of our beautiful homeland...to revisit in our hearts.

(Lights crossfade to a flashback of an idyllic scene in Vietnam with YOUNG THANH, VILLAGERS, TEACHER BINH and STUDENTS. YOUNG THANH is dressed in the traditional white Vietnamese ao dai, the uniform for students.)

"YEARNING FOR PAST SPRING"

> *THANH:*
> MY SWEET SISTER, DO YOU EVER DREAM ABOUT
> YELLOW APRICOT BLOSSOMS BY THE TERRACE IN
> PAST SPRINGS?
> I'M NOW IN THE WEST, SO FAR AWAY
> MISSING ALL VERY MUCH IN MY HEART!

VIETNAMESE CLASSMATE: Thanh! Let's get coconuts after school!

YOUNG THANH: Yes! My mom gave me money! My treat!

> *VILLAGERS:*
> MY DEAR BROTHER,
> DO YOU EVER DREAM ABOUT RED FIRECRACKERS
> ALL OVER THE CITY?

> *TRIO:*
> YOUNG WOMEN, DRESSES, AND BROCADE SHOES,
> AND FLOWING TRESSES IN THE BREEZE,

> *SECOND TRIO:*
> LEISURELY STROLLS ON EMERALD GRASS,

> *ALL:*
> TENDER MEMORIES...

> *THANH:*
> LAST NIGHT I DREAMT OF MY HOMETOWN
> SEEING MY BROTHERS AND SISTERS, SO MUCH TO
> TALK ABOUT!

VIETNAMESE NEIGHBOR (MAN): Thanh! Have you heard the news?

VIETNAMESE NEIGHBOR (WOMAN): I'm having a baby!

YOUNG THANH: Congratulations! Your first child!

VIETNAMESE NEIGHBOR (MAN): We're so happy!

> *YOUNG THANH:*
> BESIDE A BOWL OF SAVORY SPINACH SOUP

> *ALL:*
> AND LULLABIES MELODIOUS AS THE RHYTHM OF

THE SWINGING HAMMOCK...

YOUNG THANH:
OH, HOW I MISS THE THATCHED HOUSE OF OLD!
MOTHER, HAIR GRAYING, GENTLE AS THE COOL
SHADE OF COCONUT GROVES,

ALL:
FATHER, DIGNIFIED AS IN SAINTLY KINGS' ERAS,
AND GRANDMA'S TASTY MEAL THAT WARMED THE
RAINY WINTER!

TEACHER BINH: Your essay, Thanh, is excellent. Very
perceptive.

YOUNG THANH: Thank you, Teacher Binh! If it is good, it is
entirely thanks to your excellent instruction.

THANH:
AND SISTERS AND BROTHERS AND THE FRAGRANT RICE
FIELD
AND PAST ADOLESCENT LOVE LIKE A SAD REFRAIN!
ALL SWEPT AWAY BY THE BLOODY RIVER OF WAR
DISSOLVED IN THAT EVENING OF CHAOS LONG AGO.

*(Suddenly artillery fire rings out. A DEATH DANCER, with
blood red fans, moves from person to person dealing mortal
blows. People in the flashback fall, one by one, until the ground is
littered with bodies. YOUNG THANH frantically runs from body
to body, shaking them, trying to find signs of life from her loved
ones.)*

*THANH: (walking amongst fallen bodies; spoken with
underscore)*

My teacher, sweet and gentle
As the old plum tree in the village.
A bullet had punctured his heart!
Bright blood flowed, heedlessly soaking the grass!
Soft, green blades turned to red mass[1]

She was barely eighteen in years.
To the newlyweds, neighbors had just sent cheers.
Soon the promise of a new life to cherish

Mother and child, both now perished
Two innocent souls
One straying bullet![2]

On the riverbank, bodies decompose –
Where will their drifting souls go?[3]

THANH:
ALL SWEPT AWAY BY THE BLOODY RIVER OF WAR
DISSOLVED IN THAT EVENING OF CHAOS LONG AGO.

*(The sudden and severe coughs of LINH snap THANH out of her
reverie of the past, and back into the present.)*

VIETNAMESE REFUGEE #1: Thanh! Come quickly!

THANH: (going to LINH) Sweetheart! *(to others)* She's limp as a
rag. And she's got a terrible fever. I'm taking her to the
hospital. Come with me!

*(Lights fade as THANH, escorting the ailing child with the help of
one of the REFUGEES, exits swiftly. Some REFUGEES follow.)*

---

[1] Excerpt of Supreme Master Ching Hai's poem "Mourning Mr. Binh," written in 1965, Central Âu Lạc (Vietnam), originally in Aulacese (Vietnamese). From the poetry collection *Pebbles and Gold*.
[2] Excerpt of Supreme Master Ching Hai's poem "The Widower," written in 1966, Vĩnh Bình Village, Âu Lạc (Vietnam), originally in Aulacese (Vietnamese). From the poetry collection *Pebbles and Gold*.
[3] Excerpt of Supreme Master Ching Hai's poem "Dodging Bullets," written in her youth in Âu Lạc (Vietnam), originally in Aulacese (Vietnamese). From the poetry collection *Pebbles and Gold*.

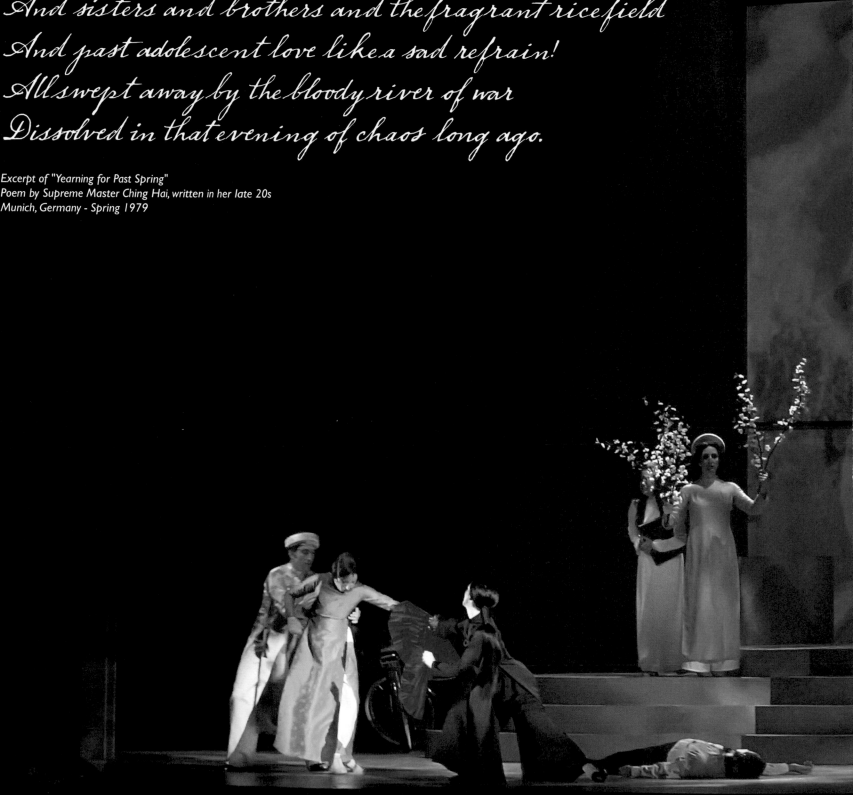

And sisters and brothers and the fragrant ricefield
And past adolescent love like a sad refrain!
All swept away by the bloody river of war
Dissolved in that evening of chaos long ago.

Excerpt of "Yearning for Past Spring"
Poem by Supreme Master Ching Hai, written in her late 20s
Munich, Germany - Spring 1979

SCENE TWO
THE HOSPITAL

DR. KLAUS BERGHOFF, dressed in a lab coat and carrying a clipboard, converses with the HEAD NURSE.

KLAUS: Nurse, I'm experiencing major resistance from Patient Steinmetz on the 9th floor vis-à-vis his post-op dietary needs.

HEAD NURSE: *(puzzled)* Steinmetz? 9th floor?

KLAUS: Affirmative. I've ordered high fiber, high protein, maximum roughage. This man needs to regain his strength.

HEAD NURSE: Let me look. *(taking his charts)* But Dr. Berghoff, Dr. Reinhardt specifically ordered sorbet and water for Steinmetz because of his gallstone procedure. It makes sense, since 9th floor is pre-op. *(looking at a different chart)* It's Steinberg – on the 11th floor – that's post-op – that needs high-cal roughage.

KLAUS: *(taking his charts back and studying them)* Let me see that... Okay...well then, mistakes can happen, granted. However, I must say that sorbet and water is not sufficient nutrition for any person regardless –

(DR. ROLF REINHARDT enters. He is tall, blonde, blue-eyed and handsome.)

ROLF: *(raising a hand)* Excuse me. If I may interject? Mr. Steinmetz, Dr. Berghoff, is, in fact, my patient, which means I am responsible for him. Including his diet before a serious procedure.

KLAUS: Yes, but as the dietician for this entire –

ROLF: I am sorry to interrupt yet again. But Mr. Steinberg, on the 11th floor, he's also my patient. And I am getting concerned about his nutritional status by now...

KLAUS: Oh. That's my job.

ROLF: Thank you.

KLAUS: Got it.

(THANH enters with LINH. A small group of REFUGEES – the group THANH was scheduled to escort to the hospital – follow. In the course of the following, they are met by NURSES, who escort them offstage, presumably to examining rooms, etc.)

THANH: Help, please. I need to see a doctor right away.

ROLF: Yes. What is it?

THANH: She's burning with fever.

KLAUS: *(rushing over and attempting to assist)* She may be suffering from calcium magnesium depletion. Is she consuming sufficient quantities of dolomite?

ROLF: Would you please resume your duties, Dr. Berghoff?

THANH: Thank you anyway, Klaus.

(KLAUS exits.)

ROLF: *(soothingly)* Take a deep breath. *(LINH coughs.)* Okay. You'll be okay. You're going to be okay. Nurse! Admit this child. Children's Care, intensive. I want a full work-up and let me know the vitals.

HEAD NURSE: Yes, Doctor. *(LINH is whisked away.)*

ROLF: *(to THANH)* She will be fine, I promise.

(One of the REFUGEES approaches THANH.)

REFUGEE #2: Thanh, I have a ringing toothache.

THANH: *(torn back from following LINH)* Oh, yes, you poor man. Doctor, can the hospital refer us to a good dentist?

ROLF: Yes, I'll take care of that.

THANH: *(taken aback)* Really?

ROLF: Well, you did ask for a good dentist, didn't you? That would be me. *(He puts on a dental headlight and proceeds to examine inside the REFUGEE's mouth.)*

THANH: You're not a – ?

 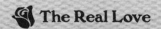

ROLF: M.D.? Of course I am. But I am, oh! *(spots something in the REFUGEE's teeth)*, but I'm also a dentist. And in my vast spare time after that, I'm chief of epidemiology. Nurse! I'll see this man momentarily in Room 4, please. *(NURSE escorts REFUGEE off.)*

THANH: You're Dr. Reinhardt!

ROLF: Guilty as charged. Rolf Reinhardt. Have we met?

THANH: No! But Elsa Mannheim is my very best friend in Germany.

ROLF: Ah yes. Elsa and I had dinner recently. I still don't know your name.

THANH: My name is Thanh.

ROLF: Thanh. It's a pleasure to meet you. *(He extends his hand. They shake.)* If I remember correctly, Elsa had a poem that was written by her best friend. That would be... you?

THANH: (laughing) I'm afraid so.

ROLF: (A beat. Then, suddenly, all-business.) So. Elsa has wonderful things to say about your work methods and I would very much like to discuss with you the refugee issue here in Germany.

THANH: I would welcome the chance to speak with you, Doctor.

ROLF: Excellent. Have dinner with me. Tonight.

THANH: Tonight?

ROLF: (He relaxes his hard-sell.) Forgive me. It would be an honor if you would be available for dinner tonight. Might you be available?

THANH: I think I would.

ROLF: I should tell you, it's my birthday.

THANH: Mine too!

ROLF: Really?

THANH: Yeah!

ROLF: Well then, we have to go someplace special!

THANH: I should tell you I'm vegetarian.

ROLF: (flummoxed; thinking hard) Hmm...

THANH: But fear not! I know where to get the best baba ganoush in all of Europe.

ROLF: Excellent! I'll pick you up at 7:30 at the Red Cross?

THANH: All right then, Doctor. *(She starts to exit but stops.)* I'm very heartened to know that you are as concerned as I am about the refugee situation.

(She exits.)

(He stares after her, wide-eyed and smitten.)

ROLF: (to the HEAD NURSE) CARLA! *(She jumps.)*

HEAD NURSE: Yes, Doctor?

ROLF: What time is my last appointment?

HEAD NURSE: (checking a datebook) Seven o'clock.

ROLF: Cancel it.

HEAD NURSE: (startled) Cancel it?

ROLF: My world has just been turned upside down!

"YOU AND THE KINGDOM"

> *ROLF:*
> IT ISN'T THE LOVELY KINGDOM
> IT IS SOMEONE HERE I COULD LOVE
> MY HEART WOULDN'T BE HERE IF SHE WERE NOT.
>
> MAYBE IT'S THE WAY THAT SHE SMILES
> MAYBE IT'S THE GENTLE TONE FROM HER LIPS
> OR THE WARMTH AND SPARKLE OF HER EYES
>
> I DON'T KNOW WHAT
> AND THE MOST BEAUTIFUL ONE ON THE PLANET
> I SEE HER EVERYWHERE
> AND THAT MOST BEAUTIFUL FACE
> THAT ENDEARING AURA
> I'M HERE, DOES SHE KNOW, I'M HERE SO NEAR
>
> IT ISN'T THE LOVELY KINGDOM
> IT IS SOMEONE HERE
> SOMEONE TO LOVE.

HEAD NURSE: Doctor, you're going to be late.

(ROLF exits.)

SCENE THREE
A RESTAURANT

THANH and ROLF are finishing up their vegetarian meal.

WAITER: Some dessert?

ROLF: No, thank you, I couldn't.

THANH: (to the WAITER) Thank you, Ferdinand. Oh! And Ferdinand – everything was delicious! *(The WAITER nods, then removes himself upstage, where he quietly stands.) (to ROLF)* Did you like your food? Isn't it interesting?

ROLF: (making a face as though he found it awful) Well, I have to admit...to be honest *(big sudden smile)*...yes!

THANH: (laughing) Why so reluctant to say so? Is it only because it is new, different, not what you're used to...?

ROLF: Good point. I mean, I find you...new...and different...and quite frankly, very interesting.

THANH: (blushing) Dr. Reinhardt –

ROLF: Please call me Rolf. I hear "Doctor Reinhardt!!" at the hospital eighteen hours a day.

THANH: (smiling) All right. *(very seriously)* Rolf, one last thing about the refugees. Imagine, if you can, being suddenly without your culture, your village, your entire...

ROLF: When do I get to hear more about you?

THANH: (ignoring his question)...We must remember that if we are to help them properly –

ROLF: Thanh, forgive me. But I feel that you are taking on too much. My heart breaks for what has happened to your people. But you – no one person – can save them all. It's impossible.

THANH: But I must try...!

ROLF: Of course you must try. But your methodology is doomed to fail. There are not enough hours in the day. I fear that you will be a burned-out woman in six months. You have to learn to simply let go.

THANH: But the love I feel for them cannot possibly burn out! I know I cannot restore everything that is lost. But their souls survive! You're a doctor, you must know what I'm talking about...?!

ROLF: I'm in the business of healing bodies, Thanh. I can't even begin to wonder what happens to their souls.

THANH: Forgive me, but that sounds a little heartless. *(Without thinking, she puts her hand on his.)* And I do not believe – in any way, that you are a completely heartless man. I saw it today, with little Linh.

ROLF: I am a scientist. A realist. You are a woman of, what? Faith?

THANH: (passionately) Yes! Of faith! The heart! Scientists! Why can't you just let the head and heart combine into one?

ROLF: (also passionately) Because Thanh, don't you see! Science is heartless! The facts are what they are. I exchanged the Church for medicine. Because faith alone never cured a kidney disease or even fixed a tooth. That little child that you brought in today...

*It was a really moving story,
and I thought the songs are really good.
They were all true to
Supreme Master Ching Hai's heart."*

TRENT KOWALIK
Tony Award-winning actor/dancer/singer

THANH: Linh.

ROLF: Linh. Suppose Linh was very ill. And there was just nothing we could do to save her. Well, sometimes sick and weak people die. You just simply have to come to accept it.

THANH: *(A beat. Then quietly)* No. I do not have to accept it. *(She rises.)* Thank you very much for dinner. And a very stimulating conversation. Will you excuse me, please? It's time for me to go.

ROLF: *(genuinely surprised)* What? So suddenly?

THANH: I'm going back to the hospital.

ROLF: At this hour?

THANH: The hour doesn't matter. I'm going to sit with Linh.

ROLF: But she'll be asleep!

THANH: All the more reason for me to be there. What if she wakes up and has no idea where she is...?

ROLF: *(THANH is almost out the door. He almost has to shout after her.)* Let me at least call you a taxi!

THANH: *(calling back; cheerfully)* No, thank you! I look forward to the walk.

ROLF: But it's freezing out, and look how dark it is!

THANH: On the contrary, there's a full moon. You must not have noticed. *(She is gone.)*

(A beat. ROLF sits silently for a moment, obviously troubled.)

ROLF: Waiter!

(The WAITER approaches the table.)

WAITER: Yes, sir.

ROLF: Check, please.

WAITER: Yes, sir. But first – some baklava?

ROLF: No, thank you. Just the check.

WAITER: Yes, sir. But first – some lingonberry cider...on the house?

ROLF: No, thank you.

WAITER: Yes, sir. But first – some advice?

ROLF: Advice?

WAITER: With your indulgence. Thanh is an extraordinary woman. One in a thousand. Perhaps one in many millions. And you are well matched. And she likes you. And you like her. Very much.

ROLF: *(blustering)* And on what do you base that brilliant observation?

WAITER: Thirty-four years in the restaurant business, sir. Forgive me, Herr Doctor. But just now, to let her go – ? A very foolish thing.

ROLF: *(A beat. He realizes the WAITER is absolutely right.)* Waiter!

WAITER: Yes, sir?

ROLF: Check, please!

WAITER: Yes, sir. *(He hands it to him. He has been concealing it behind his back.)*

ROLF: *(Thrusting money at the WAITER, he bolts for his hat and coat and heads for the door.)* And call me a very fast cab!

WAITER: Yes, sir!

(ROLF is out the door. The lights fade as the WAITER scurries to the phone.)

 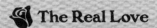

SCENE FOUR
STREETS OF MUNICH

Immediately following. THANH is walking alone under the night sky.

"MOON OF MINE"

> THANH:
> OH MOON OF MINE
> HOW SWEET YOUR SMILE
> ONLY FOR ME
> *(spoken)*
> Only for me...

(Music continues, very softly, as a kind of underscore. The lights crossfade to the children's ward of the hospital. THANH lets herself in, crosses toward LINH's bed at the far end of the room, but stops suddenly when she sees a figure, in dim light, sitting beside it. It is ROLF.)

THANH: *(sotto voce)* Dr. Reinhardt!

ROLF: *(looking up; also sotto voce)* Shhhh! She's sleeping.

THANH: What are you doing here?

ROLF: Your very smart friend Ferdinand called me a very fast cab.

THANH: *(still confused)* But I still don't –

ROLF: Shhhh! I needed to see you again, Thanh. Right away...

You were right about Linh. You were right. And I was wrong. About all of it.

THANH: I didn't mean to make you feel –

ROLF: Shhhh!

THANH: Oh Rolf...!

(With a surge of the music, THANH embraces him. They hold it for a long moment.)

THANH: *(sotto voce)* Rolf. My heart is racing.

ROLF: *(sotto voce)* How long have you been experiencing these symptoms?

THANH: They came on...very suddenly.

ROLF: A contagious condition! *(He taps his own heart.)* There's a cure, but it's risky. *(an urgent whisper)* Come outside with me!

(The lights crossfade again as ROLF and THANH cross to a corner of the stage that previously represented the street.)

ROLF: There! The moon.

THANH: *(smiling)* I thought you never noticed the moon.

ROLF: I didn't. Until I jumped in a taxi and I raced across town in the dark with my head hanging out the window looking for you! *(looking at her)* I needed the moon –

Oh moon of mine
How sweet your smile
Only for me
Oh how happy!

Can any one
See any thing
More beautiful than you!

Excerpts of "Moon of Mine"
Poem by Supreme Master Ching Hai

to help me see...don't you see? I feel like I've known you since before the moon was even born.

THANH: That long? Do you believe in reincarnation?

ROLF: Tonight, I believe only in love.

(They kiss.)

"MOON OF MINE"

THANH:
OH MOON OF MINE
HOW SWEET YOUR SMILE
ONLY FOR ME
OH HOW HAPPY!

ROLF:
NO ONE TO SEE
NO ONE TO KNOW
OUR LOVE FOR EACH OTHER
THOUGH YOU CARE FOR ALL!

BOTH:
THOUGH YOU CARE FOR ALL!

THANH:
NO ONE CAN SMILE
SO SWEET AND LONG
YOU ARE THE ONE
YOU ARE THE ONLY ONE!

ROLF:
AND WHEN I'D SUNG
YOU STAYED STILL AND HUNG
ABOVE THE MOUNTAINS

THANH:
YOU LISTENED AND DANCED
TILL MY HEART'S CONTENT...
ENDEARING AND LOVELY

BOTH:
YOU ARE THE BEAUTY
OF THE GALAXY.

THANH:
YOU SHARE THE PAIN
AND THE JOY, WITH ME!
YOU ARE THE
FRIEND OF ETERNITY.

ROLF:
YOU SHINE MY PATH
IN THE DARK
YOU SOOTHE MY HEART
WHEN I'M IN PAIN.

BOTH:
WHEN I'M IN PAIN.

(The music continues.)

(ROLF removes an engagement ring from his pocket.)

THANH: Good heavens, where did that come from?

ROLF: This belonged to my grandmother. Right before she died, she made me promise that I would always carry this around with me in my left coat pocket on the outside chance that I might find her.

THANH: Find who?

ROLF: The woman I want to marry.

THANH: That's so romantic.

ROLF: I always thought it was utterly absurd... Until now.

(ROLF gets down on one knee. He slips the ring on her finger.)

BOTH:
CAN ANY ONE
SEE ANY THING
MORE BEAUTIFUL THAN YOU!

(Lights fade.)

SCENE FIVE
WEDDING RECEPTION HALL

A WEDDING SINGER is onstage, ready to perform for THANH and ROLF's WEDDING GUESTS.

"I BELIEVE ONLY IN LOVE"

WEDDING SINGER:
BECAUSE WE ARE IN LOVE,
THE EARTH IS SO RAVISHING,
BECAUSE WE ARE IN LOVE,
THE WORLD BECOMES JOYFUL!
I BELIEVE ONLY IN LOVE

EVERYTHING ELSE ON EARTH LACKS MEANING
EVEN IF THIS WORLD IS LEVELED TO THE GROUND
I BELIEVE ONLY IN LOVE

LOVE WILL LIVE FOREVER
IN THE INFINITE UNIVERSE.
JUST TO LOVE EACH OTHER,
LOVING IS ENOUGH.
THEN OUR SOULS WILL FLOURISH, ASSURED.

OUR HEARTS WILL NOT SHIVER
DESPITE THE RAGING STORM.
I BELIEVE ONLY IN LOVE

WHEN IN LOVE,
NO ONE MINDS EXTERNAL SCENES;
EVERYWHERE IS HEAVEN
EVERYWHERE IS HEAVEN
EVERYWHERE IS HEAVEN

I BELIEVE, I BELIEVE ONLY IN LOVE, LOVE, LOVE
I BELIEVE ONLY IN LOVE, LOVE, LOVE

I BELIEVE ONLY IN LOVE, LOVE, LOVE
I BELIEVE ONLY IN LOVE, LOVE, LOVE
I BELIEVE ONLY IN LOVE, LOVE, LOVE
IN LOVE!

(Full company of WEDDING GUESTS applauds.)

FEMALE GUEST: What's more romantic than a wedding? I mean, that ceremony! – pure romance from top to bottom. Don't you agree, Ernst?

> "*It came magically together. It was meant for Supreme Master Ching Hai to be heard by the rest of the world. This is a person who has touched so many thousands of millions of people around the world. Her poetry is wonderful. She is a wonderful artist. Look at all the gifts God has given her: wonderful painter, wonderful poetess, wonderful speaker, wonderful heart. I was so moved by her, I was mesmerized actually, because she is so honest. And that is so rare in today's world to find someone like that. People around the world really must see the show. It has the strength of many great, great shows.*"

AL KASHA
Two-time Academy Award-winning composer

"SINCE WE KNEW EACH OTHER"

WEDDING GUESTS:
IN YOUR SILENT MANNER I FOUND MYSELF
IN YOUR QUIET STYLE IS REBORN MY PEACE
MANY DARK NIGHTS, SOFT AND TRANQUIL
YOUR VOICE TENDER CALMS MY MADNESS!

O LOVER OF GRAND AMOUR!
FROM REINCARNATION AND A THOUSAND PROMISES!
DO YOU STILL REMEMBER,
OUR LOVE LIVES BEFORE?...

YOUR LOVE LIKE SPRING WATER COOLS MY BURNING
HEART!
IT'S OVER, THE LONG VOYAGE,
HERE I'VE ARRIVED TO STAY.

ERNST: (Ogling a bridesmaid, he is only half-hearing his wife.)
Yes, dear. Very sweet. Top to bottom.

FEMALE GUEST: (bursts into tears) Waaaaaaahh!

ERNST: What did I do? I'm not doing anything!? What's wrong
with you?

FEMALE GUEST: (through her sobs) Nothing's wrong with me.
It's just – Thanh and Rolf – they're so beautiful! They
make me feel so – *(sob)* – happy! *(She embraces her
husband passionately.)* Oh, cake!

*WEDDING PLANNER: (appearing at the top of the stairs where
THANH and ROLF are about to make their entrance)*
Ladies and gentlemen! I give you Dr. and Mrs. Rolf
Reinhardt!

*(THANH and ROLF appear in their full wedding finery. Cheers
and applause from the GUESTS.)*

WEDDING PLANNER: (gesturing to the CONDUCTOR)
Maestro? *(The orchestra strikes up the official "First
Dance". More cheers and applause. They dance.)*

(The first dance ends. ROLF's MOTHER and FATHER approach.)

MOTHER: I wasn't going to say a word, but now I can't help
myself.

FATHER: Honey! We discussed this, this morning! We both
agreed…

MOTHER: I know, I know, I'm sorry, I'm sorry. Rolf. *(to crowd)*
Ladies and gentlemen, we're Rolf's parents, and we
promised we would not embarrass him by giving silly
speeches at his wedding.

FATHER: But now it's too late. Anyway, here goes: My son was
always a loner, pursuing his real passion: medicine. He
didn't have time for love.

MOTHER: Until he met our darling Thanh.

THANH: Thank you.

MOTHER: I'm sure Rolf has told you that love is an irrational
thing. But now he's done the most irrational thing
imaginable – he's gotten married!

FATHER: Yes, they say a man is not complete until he's married.
Then he's finished! *(He laughs uproariously at his own
joke. Silence from all other GUESTS.)*

MOTHER: Thanh, those of us who know and love Rolf see

 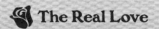

"Supreme Master Ching Hai is an incredible, incredible human being. She truly gave up the love of her life for the love of other people and other animals. And I just think she's got to be a saint really, has to be."

SHIRLEY JONES
Academy Award-winning actress/singer

something new and warm and open in his face. Especially when he looks at you. *(She hugs them both. To FATHER)* Alright, Mr. Comedy, you're on.

FATHER: Did you hear the one about...the proudest father in the world and the happiest father-in-law? *(He hugs THANH and shakes ROLF's hand.)*

MOTHER: What happened to the punchline?

FATHER: Oh, you want the punchline? Here's the punchline! *(He kisses MOTHER. Laughs and applause from WEDDING GUESTS.)*

(GRETA and RAJEEV approach THANH and ROLF.)

ROLF: Thanh! I want you to meet one of my best friends in the world. He works with me at the hospital. This is Rajeev. And his lovely wife, Greta.

GRETA: You are the most radiant bride I've ever seen.

THANH: Thank you!

GRETA: No, I mean it – your eyes: there's a Mardi Gras going on behind your eyes.

THANH: *(flattered and flabbergasted)* Really?

RAJEEV: Greta, don't terrify the poor girl on her wedding day! My wife is an artist, Thanh, a painter. She forgets to mention that before she launches into her rhapsodies over new faces.

THANH: A real artist!

GRETA: I would be so honored if you'd model for me.

THANH: The honor would be mine!

GRETA: I have a feeling we are going to get on famously. *(They embrace. ELSA approaches them.)*

ELSA: You gorgeous, gorgeous thing. Oh my God, this wedding is beautiful. You are both beautiful. Just look at you!

THANH: *(They hug.)* I wish you were wearing this dress.

ELSA: Oh now enough with that nonsense! You two are a match made in Heaven! You're just going to be so happy, and share little secrets, and joyfully climb the little ladder-of-life together, hand-in-hand, and every night when you come home from work, he'll be there, waiting for you, all tall and weary and handsome, and you'll see his stethoscope hanging on a little peg in the hallway, and he'll say to you, "Hallo, darling. How was your day?" and – Oh my GOD! I'm just so HAPPY for you I can't stand it – *(She bursts into loud tears and embraces THANH again.)*

WEDDING PLANNER: *(interrupting the hug)* Darling! Sweetie! It's time to throw the bouquet!

ELSA: Me, me, me… Right here. I'm ready. Bring it on!

(THANH throws the bouquet, which is caught by ELSA. Ad lib cheers of "Bon Voyage!" "Happy Honeymoon!" etc.)

ELSA: *(as she's dancing with various male WEDDING GUESTS who eventually leave her)*

I BELIEVE ONLY IN LOVE
I BELIEVE ONLY IN LOVE
I BELIEVE ONLY IN LOVE

(Ultimately, she is still alone. She exits. Lights fade.)

Because we are in love, the Earth is so ravishing,
Because we are in love, the world becomes joyful!
I believe only in love!

Excerpt of "When We're in Love"
Poem by Supreme Master Ching Hai
Written in her youth

SCENE SIX
THE HOSPITAL

Several weeks later. The stage is crowded with doctors and nurses and patients, and the mood is one of near-pandemonium.

KLAUS: *(at the HEAD NURSE's station)* Nurse – are you sure that Dr. Reinhardt and Thanh are coming back to work today?

HEAD NURSE: *(very busy)* That's what it says on the schedule, so it might be true.

KLAUS: Well, their honeymoon was officially over two days ago. Then there was that one-day travel from Lake Como, which would've been yesterday. Of course, one mustn't discount jet lag. Are you concerned at all about their jet lag?

HEAD NURSE: I'm nearly frantic about their jet lag. But somehow I am able to push that aside and soldier on... with my tasks at hand!

KLAUS: *(clueless)* I'm not so much concerned about Dr. Reinhardt. He wouldn't know a tropical parasite if it bit him. If only... But Thanh, oh Thanh, she's so delicate. Even though I know she's really not. You know, she'd have to have the strength of twenty women to have survived what she's been through. Even so, I made her this cake.

HEAD NURSE: You what?

KLAUS: For her jet lag. And, you know, a welcome back thing. It's flourless celery and rutabaga with a caramelized leek frosting. *(The HEAD NURSE makes a face.)* I know, do you have any idea what they serve on airplanes these days? She must have been used to eating dreck!

HEAD NURSE: Klaus, I mean Dr. Berghoff – no, I mean Klaus: I think you should back off a bit from the newlyweds. Agree, at all?

KLAUS: *(hurt and confused)* No, frankly no. I'm just trying to be...friendly.

HEAD NURSE: *(seductively)* Friendly is good. I tell you what: How about you meet me in the nurses' lounge after our next shift. And you can feed me some of that caramelized leek frosting...

KLAUS: I'm going to go put this in her locker...

HEAD NURSE: Klaus!

KLAUS: I know, don't light the candles this time! Is anybody ever going to forget that?

(KLAUS exits. THANH enters with a group of REFUGEES.)

THANH: You two, you need to go to the ENT doctor. Nurse! Could you escort them to the ENT? *(Half the group follows THANH to one side of the stage.)*

NURSE #1: Sure. *(THANH starts to cross back to assist NURSE #2.)* Thanh, when you've got a second, two more refugee buses have just arrived.

THANH: I'll be right there!

(She is approached by a REFUGEE.)

REFUGEE: Thanh! My chest is burning and my head – I think I'm going to faint! *(He collapses to the floor.)*

THANH: Nurse! We need some help here! *(NURSE #3 rushes forward to assist.)*

NURSE #2: *(shouting from the other side of the stage)* Thanh, Thanh, I need you! I don't understand a word this refugee is saying!

INTERCOM: Dr. Reinhardt – please report to Room 349.

DOCTOR: Thanh, when you have a chance – I've just come from the children's ward. Your patient Linh –

THANH: *(to NURSE #2)* I'll talk to her later. *(anxiously)* Is everything okay?

DOCTOR: *(smiling)* She's fine. But she wants to see you.

THANH: Oh! But this is not a good moment –

DOCTOR: (soothingly) Thanh, take a break. You deserve it. Go.

THANH: (A beat. A deep breath.) Thank you, Doctor.

(Lights crossfade to the area representing the children's ward. LINH is sitting up on her bed. THANH enters.)

THANH: Why, hallo! You're looking chipper!

LINH: Why are you late?

THANH: I beg your pardon?

LINH: To class!

THANH: Oh, to class! I'm very sorry, Teacher. My school bus driver got lost, you see. We ended up in an entirely different country!

LINH: What country?

THANH: I'm not entirely sure, but it might have been Zanzibar!

LINH: Is it far from here?

THANH: Pretty far. That explains why I'm so late, you see?

LINH: That's okay! But now you have to give the entire class an oral report on Zanzibar.

THANH: Oh! All right. (addressing the imaginary class of kids) Zanzibar, an island nation founded 12 million years ago by a family of Great Blue Whales. They loved to spend their summers there frolicking in the cool mountain waterfalls.

LINH: Whales don't frolic in waterfalls...!

THANH: Ah! You're just too smart for me! (She hugs LINH fiercely, both of them giggling with delight.)

(ROLF has entered, unseen by THANH and LINH. He watches silently for a moment.)

ROLF: Hallo, darling. Hallo, Linh. (He crosses to her, puts his hand on LINH's head. She gets up and hugs him, hard.)

LINH: (joyfully) Doctor, Doctor, Doctor!

ROLF: I'm so glad you're feeling better today, sweetheart. Will you excuse Thanh and me for one moment? (ROLF and THANH cross to a far corner of the stage.)

THANH: She's growing stronger every day.

ROLF: Yes, it's wonderful. But she has a test result here that I'm not at all happy about.

THANH: What is it?

ROLF: *(looking at his clipboard)* Tuberculosis. Fairly advanced and very contagious. I'm ordering her complete isolation.

THANH: Isolation...!? She needs to get out in the sunshine, see other children. Learn to forget what she's been through!

ROLF: Yes, Thanh. That would be ideal. But this is a hospital. There are other patients here that are at risk.

THANH: Maybe she could live with us…

ROLF: No. That's completely inappropriate. She'll need constant monitoring.

THANH: Will I be able to visit her?

ROLF: Yes. Under highly restricted circumstances. I cannot let you get too close.

THANH: Too close? I love her! You love her, too! Don't you?

ROLF: Of course I do. But I worry about your health, Thanh. It's too risky.

THANH: Risky? I grew up surrounded by war. I understand risk. There must be some sort of compromise for Linh...?

ROLF: No, there is no compromise in this instance. In all likelihood Linh will be fine. At which point you'll see that I was right. We're both exhausted. Let's drop the subject.

THANH: I won't. I can't.

INTERCOM: *(urgently)* Dr. Reinhardt, Room 649, stat. Dr. Reinhardt, Room 649.

THANH: *(calmer)* Rolf, I'm sorry. Let's not fight. It's just that –

ROLF: I'm not looking for a second opinion, Thanh. I'll see you tonight. *(He exits quickly.)*

THANH: *(calling after him)* Rolf – !

(THANH looks back at LINH, then stands motionless, lost in troubled thought as lights fade.)

SCENE SEVEN
STREETS OF MUNICH
Some days later. THANH alone.

"WEEKEND THOUGHTS"

THANH:
I MISSED YOU ALREADY THIS MORNING
WHEN I WOKE UP IN YOUR ARMS,
THE LAST DAY OF THE WEEKEND!
I THINK ALREADY
OF THE DAYS AHEAD
WHEN WE WILL BE "TOGETHER...
BUT IN TWO PLACES" AGAIN!
... AND WHEN I AM FAR AWAY FROM YOU
DOUBTS AND LONELINESS FLY IN THROUGH THE
WINDOW!
I JUST CAN'T THINK OF ANYTHING ELSE
BUT THROW EVERYTHING AWAY AND RUN TO YOU.
BUT DO YOU EVER
EVER WANT ME TO?

(Lights fade.)

SCENE EIGHT
ROLF'S OFFICE AT THE HOSPITAL
Immediately following. ROLF alone in his office.

ROLF: *(reading a letter)*

"Dear Doctor Darling: In recognition of our two-day anniversary of not speaking to one another, *(underscore begins)* a poem:

"I set out,
 Spreading my wings to the heavens.
 I proceed to call on you,
 The one I cherish…
 The Earth is vibrant,
 Exulting in our reunion,
 An uncommon day of happiness,
 Together as on our first meeting.
 Let us overlook
 The nights of our distress,
 Sing on full moon nights,
 Chorus on breezy days.
 Life is an aromatic flower garden,
 Oh, Mein!"[4]

Oh, mein.

(He folds up the letter, kisses it and presses it to his chest.)

ROLF: *(calling offstage)* Carla! Find someone to cover my shift! I have a date with my wife, but she doesn't know it yet!

(Blackout.)

SCENE NINE
A DISCO CLUB
THANH and ROLF are dancing.
Other people in the club dance in the background.

THANH: *(somewhat shouting; the music is very loud)* What's wrong, Fred Astaire? Can't keep up with me? *(ROLF does a defiant dance move.)*

ROLF: You can't keep up with me!

THANH: Ever tried this one?

ROLF: No problem! *(He attempts an ungainly step that twists him into an awkward shape.)* Jesus Chri – !! I'm sorry! I know, do not take in vain the name of Jesus or Buddha. Two very important men in your life. After me!

THANH: They are not men! They are Masters!

ROLF: I know, I know. Your faith keeps you grounded.

THANH: A higher power keeps all of us grounded.

ROLF: Gravity grounds me!

THANH: Without faith, people fall! Take a leap of faith with me!

(They twirl around together.)

THANH: *(laughing)* I adore you, my magnificent man of science!

ROLF: You enchant me, my poetical, passionate muse!

(Lights fade.)

---

[4] Excerpt of Supreme Master Ching Hai's poem "Visiting You," written in her youth. From the poetry collection **Pebbles and Gold**.

 The Real Love

SCENE TEN
THANH AND ROLF'S HOME
A dinner party some weeks later.
ELSA, HEINRICH, GRETA and RAJEEV are their guests.

ELSA: Thanh's meal! Delicious or what? I can't believe I love my vegetables so much. My mother would be so proud!

HEINRICH: (taking another swig from a whiskey flask that he brought) So what do you think, Rajeev? Is she a keeper? *(He makes a gesture to ELSA.)*

RAJEEV: Well, that rather depends, doesn't it?

HEINRICH: On what?

RAJEEV: On her feelings about you.

HEINRICH: Don't give me that! She's dying to marry me! *(to ELSA)* Aren't you, sugarcakes?

ELSA: Oh, stop it!

GRETA: You know, Thanh is teaching me her cooking techniques. It's fascinating. She's a brilliant teacher.

HEINRICH: (to the MEN) With my bank account she'd marry me if I was Quasimodo himself!

(THANH enters with tea.)

GRETA: Thanh, we have to set a date for my next cooking lesson. I need to learn how to make that eggplant dish. Scrumptious! Elsa! You should come too.

THANH: Thursday? At 3?

GRETA: Perfect!

HEINRICH: She's pretty. Dumb but pretty.

RAJEEV: (appalled) I, for one, do not find Miss Mannheim, by any stretch of the imagination, to be "dumb", Heinrich.

HEINRICH: Hey, don't get all women's lib on me! Women's "lip" I like to call it! – I mean it like it's flattering. She's pretty! Dumb, but pretty! Mind you I could have a

It's Master Ching Hai's poetry that I'm expressing, and David Shire's music. And I love just expressing that bit of humanity through it."

CADY HUFFMAN
Tony Award-winning actress

college graduate if I wanted one. But that's the trick, isn't it? Dumb? Smart? Skinny? Fat? Finding the perfect combination. I like 'em dumb and pretty. *(He makes another inappropriate move on ELSA.)*

ELSA: Heinrich, can you stop?

GRETA: Oh, Thanh! I almost forgot! That book we talked about last week. I brought it for you. *(She reaches into her handbag.)*

THANH: Oh, wonderful! *(taking the book and reading the cover)* Lives of the Himalayan Yogis.

HEINRICH: Is that Yogi Bear or Yogi Berra? *(He howls with laughter at his own joke.)*

ELSA: *(at her wit's end)* Yogis, Heinrich. Himalayan yogis! *(with growing sarcasm, bitterly)* But really, nobody expects you to ever have heard of such a thing. Nope. Nobody expects you to be anything, darling, but the stupid, vulgar, drunk, benighted boor that you obviously, disgustingly are!!

HEINRICH: Hey now! What kind of a thing is that to say!? How dare you say stuff like that to me! *(He starts to cross to ELSA threateningly.)*

ROLF: *(restraining him)* All right! Party's over. Goodnight, Heinrich. Goodnight, everyone. Heinrich, we're going to send you back to your home in your nice, warm bed. *(RAJEEV and ROLF hustle HEINRICH toward the door. As GRETA leaves, she touches ELSA's arm.)*

ELSA: He won't remember anything in the morning. Crazy, huh?

THANH: Why don't you stay here with us, tonight, Elsa?

ELSA: No. I think I need a little fresh air, but thanks. Thanh, I'm so sorry.

SCENE ELEVEN
STREETS OF MUNICH
Immediately after. ELSA alone in a darkened street.

"SELF CONFESSION"

> ELSA:
> I LIVE THROUGH DAYS OF DECEPTION
> PROFESSING LOVE THAT I DON'T FEEL!
> SWEET UTTERANCES FROM ROSY LIPS,
> PASSIONATE WORDS FROM AN ICE COLD HEART...
>
> I INDULGE IN MANY ILLUSIONS,
> DAY AND NIGHT, KEEPING UP WITH THE JONESES.
> THIS EPHEMERAL BODY, SKIN BURNING WITH PASSION,
> HOW I WRITHE, PLUNGING INTO THE FIRE OF LUST!!
>
> I PASS MANY SHORES, CLEAR AND MUDDY,
> WASHING MY FACE, THEN PAINTING IT AGAIN,
> DESIRING FAME, FINE HOUSES AND WEALTH
> TO ENJOY THIS LIFE, I'VE ABANDONED NOBLE IDEALS
>
> AFTER MANY STRUGGLES, I AWAKE SUDDENLY
> ASKING MYSELF, "IS THAT ALL THERE IS?"
> WHAT DOES IT MATTER, A FEW EXTRA TENS OF YEARS,
> TO CHASE FOR FAME AND GAIN WITH EFFORTS SO DEAR!
>
> WHAT SHALL I DO IN THE DAYS AHEAD,
> WHEN HAIR LOSES LUSTER AND YOUTHFUL ROSINESS FADES?
> WHEN BREATHING CEASES, IS IT DEATH OR REBIRTH?

(She goes to a phone booth and dials a number.)

ELSA: Munich 539 762, please. …Heinrich! Hey, it's Elsa! I know… I'm sorry. I'm sorry. But hey kiddo, the night's young! You want to go out for a drink or something? Great. I'll see you there.

> I ASK MYSELF IN THIS SELF CONFESSION TODAY:
> IS THIS LIFE OR IS DEATH CLOSE BY?

(ELSA hangs up. Lights fade.)

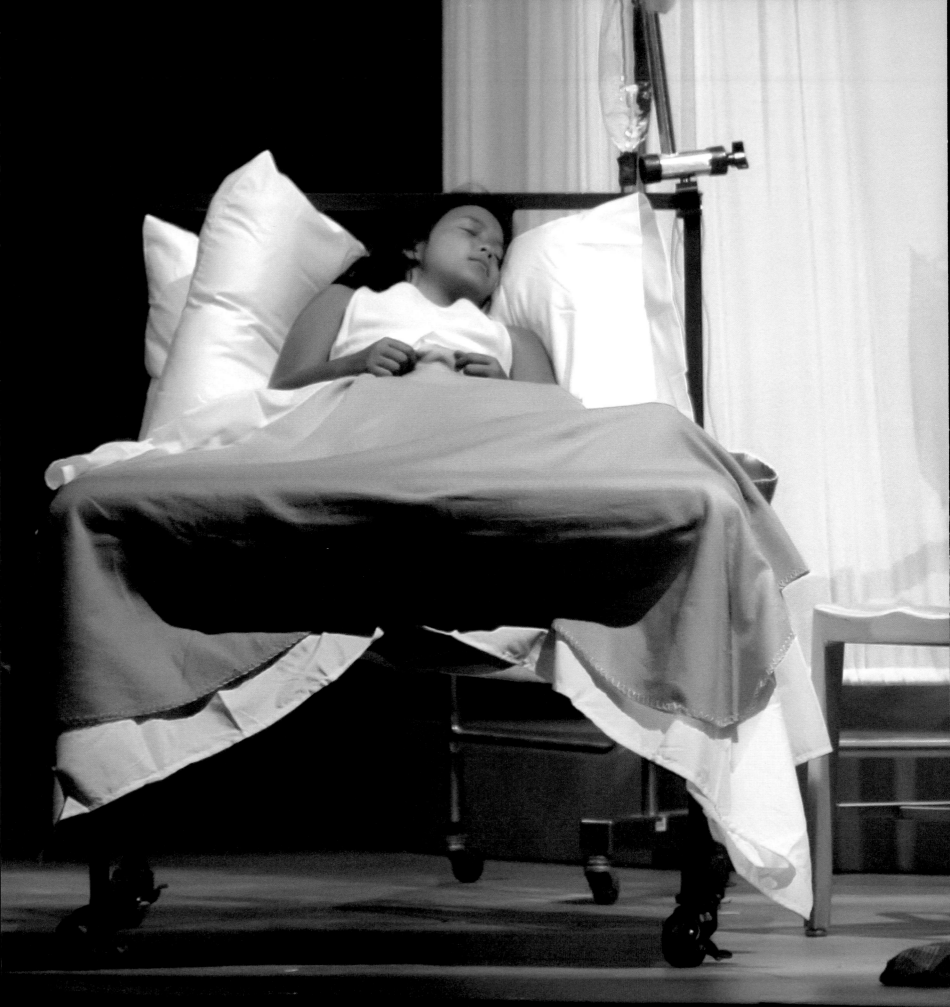

SCENE TWELVE
THE HOSPITAL

It is late at night. THANH is visiting LINH.
The lights are dim.

THANH: *(Sitting beside LINH on her bed, stroking her hair, she speaks quietly and rhythmically; LINH is half-asleep, yet restless.)* Sleep, my love. So much stronger you'll feel in the morning if now you just go to sleep. So close your eyes, my darling.

LINH: It's hard to breathe. *(She coughs.)*

THANH: I know, sweetheart. But just close your eyes, and sleep will come.

LINH: *(after a moment)* Miss Thanh, when they died, where did my mother and father and big brother go?

THANH: I don't know, sweetheart. But wherever it is, it's someplace very, very beautiful.

LINH: Like Zanzibar?

THANH: Maybe so! So just close your eyes, my darling. And dream about Zanzibar!

(LINH is at last asleep. THANH kisses her forehead and tiptoes away.)

THANH: *(urgently and passionately)* How I wish I had the answer for her! How I wish I had the answer to all the suffering in this life. I work, I sleep, I work some more. And always I am praying. Putting the pain in my writing, giving my love to the children, the lost ones, every last one of them! But it isn't enough. Nothing changes the suffering.

Dear God! Show me a sign You exist. Dear Buddha! Let me see You, let me know Your compassion, Your power. Because I need strength, God! I need strength. Not for me, but for Linh. But why the endless suffering? Where is the everlasting remedy? I know in my heart there IS one! But where is it? Won't You show me a sign?

(Lights fade.)

SCENE THIRTEEN
GRETA'S STUDIO

GRETA is painting; THANH, holding a red rose,
is modeling for her.

GRETA: *(Pausing in her work, she stares at THANH for a long moment; THANH, turned away, does not notice GRETA's gaze.)* I think we should stop for today.

THANH: *(startled)* Why?

GRETA: What's going on?

THANH: Nothing.

GRETA: Thanh! It's my business to see things in people's faces. Something pretty serious is going on.

THANH: *(A beat; then she drops all guard.)* Linh isn't getting any better. In fact, she's getting worse.

GRETA: I'm so sorry.

THANH: I'm scared she's going to die.

GRETA: Of course you are.

THANH: I feel my faith is faltering. I feel lost.

GRETA: Ever since I was a little girl, I wanted to be a painter. Art was my enchantment. But it was "only" a dream. So I grew up, I got practical, and I went to med school – because my father was a doctor. But also because medicine was important, unlike, say, art. I met Rajeev. We fell in love. We got married, and we both started practicing. But then a couple of years later, this little voice started waking me up in the middle of the night telling me that I needed to be painting. I ignored that little voice. But it got louder, more adamant. And then one day I woke up and I knew – I simply knew – I had to go to Paris.

(Toward the end of GRETA's talking, RAJEEV has entered carrying a tray with a plate of strudel, a pot of steeping chai, and three cups.)

THANH: Paris! What did you think of that, Rajeev?

RAJEEV: *(with mock horror)* Absolutely opposed! Hated the idea!

GRETA: So, he stayed home. But I had to honor something that felt bigger than myself, Thanh. A spirit. That little voice! I needed to go to Paris to study with the living masters of my art. Otherwise – I would be betraying something in my soul.

THANH: You were very brave to go.

GRETA: Honestly? Yes. I was. But let me tell you the best part: Yes, going to Paris, I became a better artist than I otherwise possibly could have been. But I became a better person. Thanh, tell me what's wrong.

THANH: *(in turmoil)* I don't know! I'm not a painter like you. I'm a – I don't know what I am!

GRETA: Well, you're a deeply spiritual woman.

THANH: I know, I know it sounds blasphemous, but – God and Buddha – they seem...so far away.

RAJEEV: *(pouring the tea)* My country, Thanh – India – India has been a crucible of suffering for centuries. We have struggled with your question more than most: Where is God, in the midst of all...this...suffering...?

THANH: And?

RAJEEV: Perhaps because of that, a few, very few, wise Masters have learned the answers to that elusive question. And live to enlighten others.

THANH: Living Masters. In India?

(RAJEEV simply nods. The phone rings. RAJEEV excuses himself to answer it.)

THANH: I don't know if I will have the courage to go. You were very strong.

GRETA: I had the courage to take the first step. That's all I had.

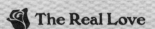

*There's a great diversity in her poems.
They're contemplative, they're humorous,
they're describing the world situation.*

*Sometimes when I was reading
Supreme Master's poems,
they just came out with a musicality.
Supreme Master's poems just sing.*

It's much deeper than a lot of lyrics go."

FRANK EVANS
Award-winning writer & lyricist

When you're in the rehearsal room with the whole cast and crew, it reminds me of when I was in Les Misérables. *It's just massive.*

All the songs are poems by the Supreme Master Ching Hai, and the songs are beautiful. To hear the ensemble singing everything in full harmony full out gives you goosebumps. It's really beautiful."

DAISY EAGAN
Tony Award-winning actress

"SEARCH HIGH AND LOW"

GRETA:
SEARCH HIGH AND LOW
FOR A LITTLE LOVE,
SEARCH HIGH AND LOW
FOR A LITTLE LOVE!
TO BESTOW ON ALL BEINGS
IN ALL CORNERS OF EXISTENCE!

RIDING COLOSSAL WAVES
FLYING THROUGH GRAYING FORESTS
CHARGING INTO THE FEROCIOUS WIND
CROSSING THE STORMY SKY!

SEARCH HIGH AND LOW
FOR A LITTLE LOVE,
SEARCH HIGH AND LOW
FOR A LITTLE LOVE!

YOU HAVE TO BREATHE
THE AIR OF HEAVEN
YOU HAVE TO GO
WHERE THE WIND BLOWS

FLY WITH THE BIRDS
RISE WITH THE SUN
LOOK INTO THE HEART OF A FLOWER
AND FIND GOD THERE.

SEARCH HIGH AND LOW
FOR A LITTLE LOVE,
SEARCH HIGH AND LOW
FOR A LITTLE LOVE!

RAJEEV: (entering) Thanh, that was Rolf on the phone. He
thinks perhaps you should meet him at the hospital.

THANH: Is it Linh?

RAJEEV: Yes, it's Linh.

THANH: Is everything okay?

RAJEEV: You should go. Go now, Thanh. *(He helps her with her
coat.)*

(With a quick look of apology and gratitude to her friends,

*THANH is out the door. GRETA and RAJEEV exchange a worried look.
Lights fade.)*

SCENE FOURTEEN
THE HOSPITAL

Minutes later. A gurney is rolled across the stage. It is LINH being rushed into surgery. THANH enters. She waits anxiously in a corridor. Several beats. ROLF enters, in operating scrubs. Their eyes meet, he shakes his head. They embrace. Both are devastated.

ROLF: *(fighting tears)* I couldn't save her, Thanh. I'm so sorry.

THANH: No one blames you, darling.

ROLF: It almost felt like she were...ours. Our own daughter.

THANH: Yes.

(They are both in tears.)

ROLF: Let's start our own family, Thanh. Let's have our very own child.

THANH: That's a beautiful idea. But there is something I need to tell you. I must go to India.

ROLF: India?

THANH: Come with me. I feel it! It's my calling. I must go!

ROLF: You're not thinking clearly, Thanh! The way to cope with Linh is to move ahead, not run away to India!

THANH: This is not running away! What is the meaning in her death? Her suffering? I must find out! Come with me, Rolf! You spent ten years to become a physician. I'm only asking for two.

ROLF: No! My work! And I don't want you to go, either. I, I – need you here beside me.

THANH: *(holds onto his arm)* I need your blessings for this.

ROLF: You're asking for blessings from a man who has no faith?

THANH: That's not true! You said you believe in the power of love!

ROLF: I believe in the power of my love for you.

THANH: Then how about this: that God loves us all? That if we love each other as strongly as that we can conquer anything. Even disease!

ROLF: This is your path, Thanh. It's not mine.

THANH: But it's our lives.

ROLF: I love you, Thanh. But my life is here.

(Music underscoring begins.)

THANH: *(A long beat; then, quietly)* Then I must go alone.

ROLF: Please don't do this. I don't want to lose you.

THANH: I have no choice.

"FOR THE ONE WHO STAYED BEHIND"

THANH:
WHEN YOU COME HOME,
THERE WILL BE ONLY GRASS AND FLOWERS
GREETING YOUR FOOTSTEPS!

ROLF:
THE GARDEN SHEDS HER EVENING DEW,
THE HOUSE BOWS WEIGHED DOWN IN LONELINESS,
MURMURING FAREWELL!

THANH:
EVEN IF MY HEART WAS MADE OF STONE
AND MY FEELINGS ALL OF BRASS,

BOTH:
I WOULD SOFTEN AND MELT
AS I FEEL THE PAIN I LEFT YOU!

THANH:
BUT BELOVED ONE!
I CAN NO LONGER STAY IN DARKNESS,
SURRENDERING TO IGNORANCE AND MISERY.

ROLF:
I KNOW YOU'VE BEEN SUFFERING IN GOLDEN BOND
LONGING TO BE FREE

BOTH:
I LOVE YOU AS I LOVE MYSELF

THANH:
LIKE MY LOVE FOR THIS GREAT EARTH, ITS
MOUNTAINS AND RIVERS

ROLF:
I BOW TO YOU IN AWE OF YOUR DEEP LOVE!
WHO KNOWS WHEN WE WILL EVER MEET AGAIN–

THANH:
PRAISED BE THE DIVINE WHOSE LIGHT GUIDES MY WAY,
AND PROTECTS YOU IN YOUR LONELY DAYS.

ROLF:
WHY WERE WE BORN IN THIS WORLD OF WOE
WHERE I MUST PINE AND WHERE YOU, MY LOVE,
HAVE TO TASTE SORROW!?

THANH:
PLEASE LIFT YOUR HEART OUT OF THE BLUE WEB
SO MY MIND WILL ALSO BE LIGHTENED WHEN WE
ARE APART.

ROLF:
YOU'RE LEAVING, REACHING FOR HEAVEN ABOVE
VOWING TO LEVEL OUT ALL UPHEAVALS IN LIFE!

THANH:
ONE DAY I'LL BE ENLIGHTENED, BRING
ILLUMINATION TO THE WORLD,

BOTH:
I WANT TO BE TOGETHER FOR ETERNITY...
THOUGH FOR NOW WE'LL PART TO WALK TWO
SEPARATE PATHS
WHO WILL PROTECT THE ONE WHO STAYS BEHIND?
WHO WILL PROTECT THE ONE WHO GOES AFAR?

(Lights fade.)

 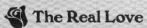

It was really a once-in-a-lifetime presentation. There's going to be a huge ripple effect from this. I had tears coming down a few times just to see the poignancy of the love that she shared with not only the man who was her husband, but for the Vietnamese people and for the animals, for the whole human family."

WILL TUTTLE, PH.D (Vegan)
Best-selling author

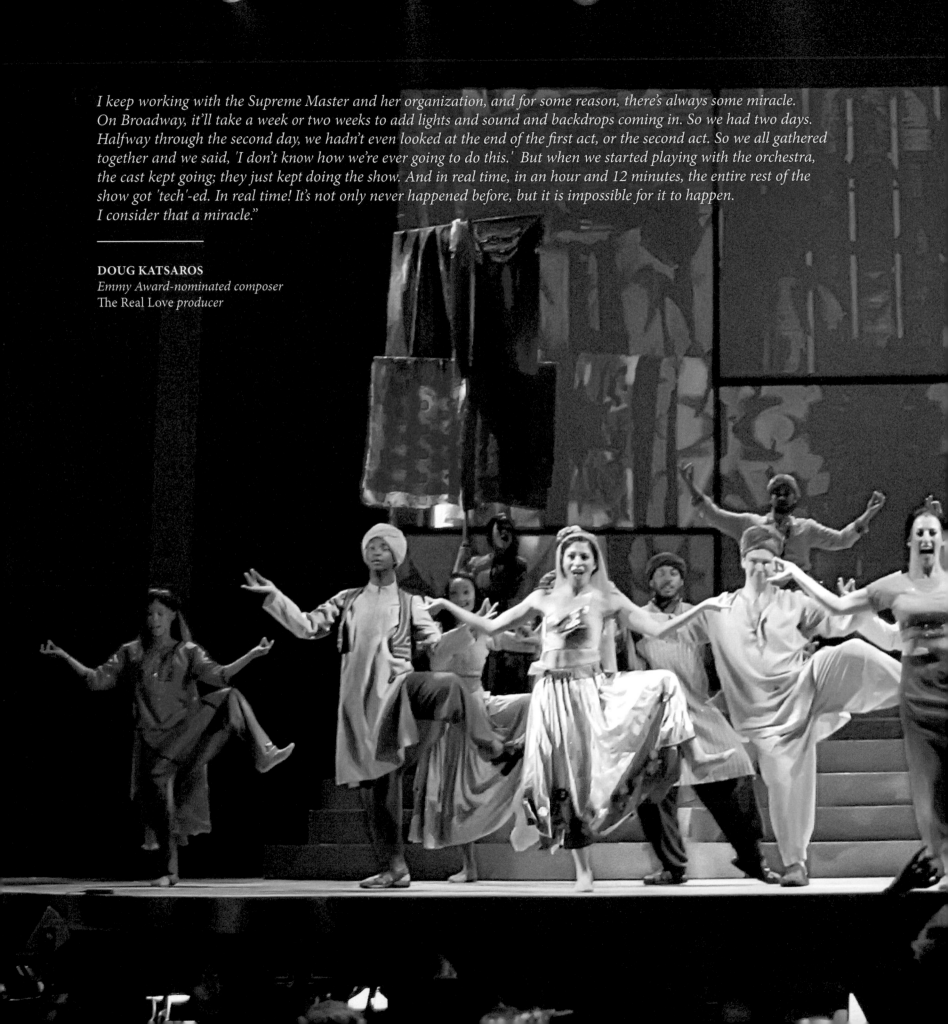

I keep working with the Supreme Master and her organization, and for some reason, there's always some miracle. On Broadway, it'll take a week or two weeks to add lights and sound and backdrops coming in. So we had two days. Halfway through the second day, we hadn't even looked at the end of the first act, or the second act. So we all gathered together and we said, 'I don't know how we're ever going to do this.' But when we started playing with the orchestra, the cast kept going; they just kept doing the show. And in real time, in an hour and 12 minutes, the entire rest of the show got 'tech'-ed. In real time! It's not only never happened before, but it is impossible for it to happen. I consider that a miracle."

DOUG KATSAROS
Emmy Award-nominated composer
The Real Love *producer*

ACT TWO

SCENE ONE

DELHI, INDIA

Some weeks later. As the lights come up, a motley assortment of Indian people in native attire portrays a bustling city.

"WELCOME TO INDIA"

INDIAN LOCALS:
SARIS!
COWS!
TEMPLES, TEMPLES
HERE COME MORE COWS! HERE COME MORE COWS!
RICKSHAWS, BUSES, BIKES AND CABS
AND CROWDS AND CROWDS OF PEOPLE.

FIGS!
CANDLES, CANDLES
HERE COME MORE COWS, HERE COME MORE COWS!
ROTIS, CURRIES, BELLS AND GONGS
AND BLAZING, BLAZING HEAT.

ASHRAMS
BEADS
SADHUS, SADHUS
EV'RY BELIEF, EV'RY BELIEF
VISHNU, KRISHNA
AND PILGRIMS OFF THE BUS.

"THE GOD SEEKER"

THANH: (bursting through the crowd)
FINALLY I'LL FIND WHAT I'VE BEEN SEARCHING FOR
CASTING ASIDE RICHES AND COMFORT
AND OH!
I'LL SEARCH FOR GOD EVERYWHERE!

FINALLY I'LL FIND WHAT I'VE BEEN SEARCHING FOR
ABANDONING LIFE LIKE A ROADSIDE INN
AND OH!
I'LL SEARCH FOR ILLUMINATION EVERYWHERE!

THANH: (to LOCALS)
WHERE'S THE SOURCE OF THE GANGES?

LOCALS:
STRAIGHT AHEAD!

THANH:
THE TEMPLE AT BENARES?

LOCALS:
STRAIGHT AHEAD!

THANH:
THE HIMALAYAN PEAKS?

LOCALS:
STRAIGHT AHEAD!

THANH:
STRAIGHT AHEAD?
STRAIGHT AHEAD?
IS EVERYTHING STRAIGHT AHEAD??

FINALLY I'LL FIND WHAT I'VE BEEN SEARCHING FOR
LEAVING BEHIND MY POSSESSIONS AND BELOVED
AND OH!
EVERYTHING'S WAITING HERE FOR ME!

(As the crowd disperses, THANH tries to get the attention, one after the other, of local passersby as they rush past. They all ignore her, indicate they have no idea what she's talking about, point vaguely into the distance, or say, "Straight ahead!" Finally, she approaches an OLD WOMAN who is peddling kindling on the street.)

THANH: Excuse me, please. I need directions, and –

OLD WOMAN: How can I help you? You are a pilgrim.

THANH: You are observant. I'm trying to find my way to Rishikesh. Do you know the way? And please don't say "straight ahead".

OLD WOMAN: In the foothills of the Himalayas.

THANH: Yes!

OLD WOMAN: I can tell you the path on foot – it is that way. *(She gestures.)*

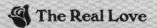

I've been searching for the Buddha everywhere
Casting aside riches and comfort,
Leaving behind my possessions and beloved!

Excerpt of "The God Seeker"
Poem by Supreme Master Ching Hai, written in her early 30s
McLeod Ganj, India

THANH: *(appreciative, reaches into her pocket)* Thank you! I am so grateful to you. Can I offer you something for your kind assistance...?

OLD WOMAN: Are you in need of some kindling for your stove?

THANH: Well, no, but –

OLD WOMAN: Then best it is saved for someone who does.

THANH: *(touched, puts her money away)* Of course.

OLD WOMAN: I would like to offer you something, however. *(She picks up her walking stick.)* You will need this.

THANH: No, I couldn't possibly – *(a beat)* Thank you so much. *(She takes the stick and bows to the OLD WOMAN. When she rises again, there is an enormous smile on her face.)*

OLD WOMAN: I'm going to call you Smiling Step.

THANH: Smiling Step?

OLD WOMAN: Yes. If only you could see your face! *(She exits.)*

(THANH continues on her journey and crosses to another street. A GIRL, carrying a large basket of flowers, trips and falls to the ground. THANH rushes to help her. The GIRL slaps THANH on the hand.)

THANH: *(startled)* Oh! I'm so sorry. I didn't mean to –

GIRL: Do not touch me! *(She quickly walks away.)*

(A SADHU approaches THANH, chuckling.)

SADHU: She's of the Brahmin caste, my dear. Only those of the same caste are allowed to touch her.

THANH: But how is one to know – ?

SADHU: Very difficult, pilgrim. My advice: not to touch anyone.

THANH: Thank you, Guruji.

SADHU: India is full of wonders and mysteries. Some dangerous. Some not. You are traveling alone?

THANH: Yes.

SADHU: That I would categorize as dangerous.

THANH: It's just that I'm in a great hurry to get to the Himalayas.

SADHU: Ah! So it is enlightenment you seek?

THANH: Yes. With every fiber of my soul.

SADHU: You want to learn to walk on water and fly in the air?

THANH: No, I'm not looking for mystical powers. I want to help people – and I need enlightenment to know how best to do that!

SADHU: *(smiling)* Beware, young woman in a hurry! You cannot do this alone. You will need help. A friend. A guide. For example, the Himalayas are bitterly cold. Have you learned tumo heat?

THANH: No. I don't even know what that means!

SADHU: Generating warmth from the solar plexus. The only way to survive.

THANH: *(a little anxiously)* Oh, I thought if I kept walking... the exercise would keep me warm... I have so much to learn.

SADHU: But my dear, do not make the mistake of falling into despair! I knew from the first moment I saw you, you were a special one. So many of my students are chasing physical attainments, not truly searching for the Truth. I've traveled to every corner of India, learned with great masters and attained great enlightenment. *(a courtly little bow)* Goodbye. And good luck. *(Begins to walk away.)*

THANH: Wait, Guruji! You said "students". You are a teacher! I would very much like to learn your path.

SADHU: We welcome you. My temple is in the mountains on the other side of the river. Too far to walk.

THANH: I will gladly pay for your bus fare, if you'll allow me.

(She reaches for her satchel that is carried close to her body.)

SADHU: I accept. Come, let us begin our journey.

(Lights fade.)

It's a huge production! There was a beautiful song that
the character of Master Ching Hai sang, about 'What do I do?
My faith is shaking and I don't know what I'm supposed to do'
('P.S. Till Tomorrow'). It's lovely."

KRISTIN BAUER (Vegetarian)
Actress (True Blood)

SCENE TWO
THE SADHU'S TEMPLE

Many hours later. Night. A group of MEN drinking from gourds or jugs and dancing drunkenly. They are disheveled, slovenly, unshaven.

MEN:
IN OUR TEMPLE
HERE IS THE TRUTH, HERE IS THE TRUTH
IF YOU WANT ENLIGHTENMENT,
WE'VE GOT IT HERE FOR YOU.

SADHU: My disciples! I return. *(There is a desultory effort by the MEN to stand straight and appear presentable.)* And I bring with me our newest pilgrim! This is Thanh. Welcome her!

(The MEN grunt their greetings. THANH nods.)

SADHU: *(to THANH)* Forgive their rough manners, my child. They are overly stimulated from a long day of study and prayer. *(to a MAN, roughly)* Something to drink! Food! *(to THANH)* You are hungry?

THANH: Famished, actually!

SADHU: Excellent! To nourish the soul, one must not neglect the body. But first, a light repast, something cool to drink. A little wine, perhaps?

THANH: Just a cup of water would be perfect.

SADHU: A cup of water… Ah, yes, a cup of water. My young student – come here. For the young lady, it shall be a cup of water, but for her, it shall be a special Elixir of Welcome.

MAN: *(A confused beat. Finally, his eyes widen in understanding.)* Ah yes, Master!

(During the following, the MAN ladles water into a cup and adds a pinch of powder from a tiny tin box.)

SADHU: Later, you shall have my room, there, in the back. I shall sleep here, with the others.

I'm tired!
Heartbroken.
Have no more patience.
After all, I'm only a frail mortal, You know it!
I quit.

P.S. Till tomorrow.

Excerpt of "P.S. Till Tomorrow"
Poem by Supreme Master Ching Hai
Written in her early 30s

It's a unique experience because I've written a lot of musicals. But normally, you sit in a room with your collaborators, the book writer, the lyricist. And this, we all were working separately. The only common denominator was the script and the Supreme Master's wonderful work.

It's a wonderful story for a musical, actually. It's like none other that I've ever seen. And that's what you want for a show, something that's surprising."

—————————

DAVID SHIRE
Two-time Grammy & Academy Award-winning composer

THANH: Oh, I couldn't. I wouldn't want to –

SADHU: Nonsense. Nonsense, nonsense. *(The MAN returns with a cup of water for THANH and hands it to the SADHU. The SADHU hands her the cup and slips his arm around her shoulder; picks up a glass himself.)* To your health! *(He drinks; she hesitates, sensing there is something amiss in the water in her cup.)*

THANH: Thank you.

SADHU: I have so much to learn about you, my child. Your spiritual journey thus far. I want to know all about it. Hold nothing back. If I am to be your teacher, you must trust me.

THANH: *(inching away from him)* I have questions. Many, many questions.

"P.S. TILL TOMORROW"

THANH:
YOUR DOOR IS FOREVER FORBIDDEN
EVERY TIME I APPROACH
IT SHUTS ALOOF AND COLD!
THE CURTAINS ARE DRAWN.
I KNOW YOU ARE IN THE PALACE.
JUST CAN'T OPEN THE DOOR.
I THINK ONE DAY I'LL BRING ALONG A BIG HAMMER!

I'M TIRED!
HEARTBROKEN.
HAVE NO MORE PATIENCE.
AFTER ALL, I'M ONLY A FRAIL MORTAL, YOU KNOW IT!
I QUIT.
P.S. TILL TOMORROW.

GOD! DO YOU HAVE EARS AT ALL?
YOU MUST!
IN ORDER TO HEAR MY DESPERATE CALL.
I THINK...
I'LL BUY A PAIR OF HUMAN EARS FOR YOU TOMORROW.

IN CASE YOU'VE LOST THE HUMAN HEART,
PLEASE TAKE MINE.
SO YOU MAY SYMPATHIZE

WITH ALL MY FELLOW BEINGS ON THE SAME BOAT,
WHO LONG FOR NIRVANA,
BUT ALL THEY KNOW IS SORROW.

HERE ARE MY HUMAN EYES OFFERED WITH GLADNESS,
PLEASE WEAR THEM 24 HOURS A DAY.
SO YOU MIGHT SEE
HOW I'VE BECOME SO WEARY
WALKING THIS PATH SO LONELY,
FOREVER SEARCHING FOR A GLIMPSE
OF YOUR BEAUTY...YOUR BEAUTY.
FOR A GLIMPSE OF YOUR BEAUTY.

I'M TIRED!
HEARTBROKEN.
HAVE NO MORE PATIENCE.
AFTER ALL, I'M ONLY A FRAIL MORTAL, YOU KNOW IT!
I QUIT.
P.S. TILL TOMORROW...
TOMORROW...
TILL TOMORROW.

(As the song progresses, the MEN become more and more drunk, dancing about THANH. At one point, their jug is handed to THANH, who takes the opportunity to pour the drugged water from her cup into the jug. The MEN continue to drink from it and one by one pass out, asleep on the floor, including the SADHU. At the conclusion of the song, THANH gathers her belongings and quietly flees out the front door to freedom.)

(The MEN all wake up and realize THANH is gone.)

SADHU: Where? Where is she? You idiots! She's gotten away! After her!

(They run off. Sound of thunder.)

SCENE THREE
THE FOREST

Some minutes after. THANH enters, running. She is breathing heavily. Occasional thunder is heard.

THANH: *(after a moment, facing heavenward)* Dear God! What, pray, am I supposed to learn from that! For this I have left my warm and safe home; my beautiful and beloved husband!?? *(Breathes some more.)* Lord, You know I put my faith in You… But where are You?

(Voices and footsteps of MEN approaching. Flashlights indicate they are searching the forest. THANH quickly gathers her things, hesitates a moment trying to decide which way to run. When suddenly – a VOICE!)

VOICE: Thanh!

THANH: What? *(Looking about, she cannot tell where the VOICE is coming from.)*

VOICE: Thanh!!

THANH: Who's calling me!?!

VOICE: I'm over here! It's KLAUS!

THANH: *(seeing him at last)* KLAUS!!??

KLAUS: *(He is wearing a full Tugboat Annie-style rain slicker.)* Klaus Berghoff! This is the craziest miracle ever! Running into you in India! Hundreds of thousands of square miles, hundreds of millions of people, what are the odds – !?

THANH: *(a fierce whisper)* KLAUS!! Shush!!

KLAUS: *(whispering)* What are the odds?

THANH: I've just escaped from a bunch of dangerous con men!

(Voices and flashlights come closer.)

SADHU: *(offstage)* She can't possibly have gotten much further than this! Spread out, boys!

(KLAUS and THANH scramble to hide.)

THANH: Give me your coat.

KLAUS: Here, you want binoculars too?

THANH: I don't need that.

(THANH curls down on the ground and uses KLAUS' coat to conceal herself, making herself look like a rock with a coat strewn on top.)

KLAUS: Okay. Okay, they're getting real close, we should… Thanh? Thanh? Where did you go? Thanh…?

THANH: *(whispers loudly from under the coat)* I'm down here.

(KLAUS quickly sits down and leans against the "rock" as the SADHU and his MEN enter.)

ONE OF THE MEN: Hey! What's this?

SADHU: *(He gives a kick to KLAUS.)* Another pilgrim, no doubt. You! Idiot! Wake up! *(KLAUS, feigning sleep, groans and raises his head.)* We're looking for a woman – small, attractive, in a hurry. Have you seen her?

KLAUS: No. *(The SADHU is about to sit on the "rock" and KLAUS quickly shouts out, causing the SADHU to freeze in his position)* I mean… YES! Heading THAT way! *(He points in the opposite direction where the MEN were headed.)*

SADHU: *(quickly bolts up)* That way, boys!

(The SADHU and MEN run off.)

THANH: *(whispering, still hidden beneath the coat)* Are they gone?

KLAUS: Not yet…

THANH: I don't hear anything.

KLAUS: Okay, now they're gone.

(KLAUS scrambles to his feet and THANH uncovers herself. They look at each other and explode into near-hysterical laughter.)

THANH: KLAUS! You're my hero! You were brilliant!

KLAUS: (puffed with his manly heroism) I was pretty good, wasn't I? Listen, are you all right?!

THANH: I'm fine! Klaus, I think you just saved my life.

KLAUS: (beaming) You know what, we've got to get out of here!

THANH: Yes, please. But where?

KLAUS: There was an ashram not too far back. I think.

THANH: You think?

KLAUS: Well, maybe it was a little far back. You see, I've been on a bird-watching expedition, and –

THANH: Perhaps we can find it together. I have to ask – I mean, it is a miracle you're here, but what on earth are you doing in India?

KLAUS: Same as you, Thanh! I'm just broadening my circle of spiritual understanding! You know, when I got fired from the hospital in Munich, I thought to myself, whoa! This is not good! But then, I saw this as the opportunity that it could be –

THANH: We have to go. *(They go.)*

(Lights fade.)

SCENE FOUR
MUNICH, GERMANY
Night. ROLF is alone on a bridge over the river.

"DO YOU MISS ME, DARLING"

ROLF:
WHEN YOU'RE THERE
AND I AM HERE,
I MISS YOUR EYES, EVER SPARKLING.
DO YOU MISS ME, DARLING?
DO YOU MISS ME, DARLING?

LONGING FOR SOMEONE FAR AWAY,
LIVING AN EMPTY LIFE,
I MISS YOUR SOFT AND BEAUTIFUL LIPS.
DO YOU MISS ME, DARLING?
DO YOU MISS ME, DARLING?

THE RIVER CONTINUES FLOWING, INDIFFERENT,
THE LONELY ROSEBUSH IS CHEERLESS.
I DREAM OF OUR GLORIOUS TIME TOGETHER.
HOLDING THE SINGLE PILLOW.

SEAGULLS ARE FLYING LOW,
BOATS TOSS AND TURN.
THE BAY THIS EVENING SEEMS SO DISTANT.
DO YOU MISS ME, DARLING?
DO YOU MISS ME, DARLING?

(As the music fades, ELSA emerges from the shadows.)

ELSA: What a touching scene! A man, all alone very late at night on a lonely bridge. Singing pretty songs...to the moon?

ROLF: Hallo, Elsa. You startled me.

ELSA: Oh, I'm sorry. I thought doctors were unflappable. But please don't fly away, like all the pigeons do whenever I come near. I'm actually grateful for the company. It's usually pretty empty out here.

ROLF: You come here often?

ELSA: Lately I do.

ROLF: I see.

ELSA: *(A beat.)* You miss her terribly. Don't you?

(ROLF remains silent.)

ELSA: And what have you heard? Has Thanh written to you?

ROLF: A note from the airport saying she arrived safely.

ELSA: I'm sure she misses hearing from you.

ROLF: My life here? – so much the same. Nothing significant to report in any case.

ELSA: *(moving closer)* Except for the terrible...loneliness, Rolf? Especially...late at night?

(ELSA puts her arms around his neck and is about to kiss him. He stops her. She pulls away.)

ELSA: *(Profoundly humiliated, she tries to make a joke.)* Oh, wow! Wait'll my therapist hears about this: Oh boy, it has gotten so bad that I've taken to making out with marble statues in the middle of Munich in the middle of the night!

ROLF: *(very seriously)* Elsa, you know how much in love with my wife I am.

ELSA: *(A short beat as this sinks in.)* Oh! I'm a horrible person! *(She starts to cry.)*

ROLF: No, no, no, please…

ELSA: *(through her sniffles)* Rolf, oh God, I've something to show you. It's a letter from India. It's from Klaus. Remember Klaus? From the hospital? Anyway, he and I have become penpals. Well, he and Thanh, they are staying in an ashram, somewhere. So she's okay. There's a return address if you'd like to write her. *(She hands the letter and the picture to ROLF, who shows a big sigh of relief.)* Or why don't you just go? What are you doing standing around here?

ROLF: I've been wanting to find her. Now I can. Thank God!

(ROLF turns to leave and is stopped by ELSA.)

 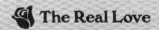

ELSA: Rolf, please give my love to Thanh. And you will never mention what happened here tonight. Ever...? *(He nods.)* Okay, goodnight! Goodbye. *(She exits quickly.)*

(ROLF, still staring at the letter and the picture, suddenly presses the picture and letter to his heart.)

ROLF:
AS NIGHTS PASS AND DAYS GO BY
I MISS ONLY YOU, ALL THE TIME!
DO YOU MISS ME, DARLING?

(Lights fade.)

SCENE FIVE
THE GANGES RIVERBANK

THANH sits by the side of the Ganges River.
We hear the sound of river water flowing.

"ON THE RIVERBANK"

THANH:
I LOVE TO SIT ON THE RIVERBANK
LISTENING TO THE SOUND OF WATER
AND THE BIRDS.

I LOVE TO SIT ON THE RIVERBANK
LOOKING AT THE FLOWING WATER
AND HEAR THE SONGS WITHIN...

YOU MAKE MY LIFE FLOWING
LIKE THE RIVER WATER.
THEN TOMORROW WE'LL REACH THE SEASHORE...

I LOVE TO SIT ON THE RIVERBANK
REMEMBERING THE TEARS IN YOUR EYES
WHEN YOU SPOKE OF
THE SUFFERING IN THIS WORLD.

YOU MAKE MY LIFE FLOWING
LIKE THE RIVER WATER.
THEN TOMORROW WE'LL REACH THE SEASHORE...

I LOVE TO SIT ON THE RIVERBANK
REMEMBERING THE TEARS IN YOUR EYES
WHEN YOU SPOKE OF
THE SUFFERING IN THIS WORLD.

(Lights fade.)

SCENE SIX
DELHI, INDIA

ROLF approaches various Indian locals.

ROLF: (holding up a photo of THANH at the post office) Have you seen this small Vietnamese woman?

POSTAL WORKER: Oh, she left here already.

ROLF: Where did she go?

POSTAL WORKER: Straight ahead!

ROLF: (rushes to a bank) Have you seen the woman in this photo?

BANK TELLER: She looks familiar. I believe she went that way.

ROLF: Thanks! *(hurries off)*

ROLF: (at an ashram) I'm searching for my wife. Is she at this ashram?

GOOD SADHU: No, she has left for Rishikesh. But my son, better you should search for your soul.

ROLF: Ah! My soul is in Rishikesh! *(runs off excitedly)*

(Lights fade.)

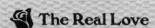

"I have played some amazing parts and this would have to be at the top. It's a real story, I'm playing a real person here.

And it's been such a wonderful journey for me BECAUSE FOR THIS PARTICULAR PART, I'VE TURNED VEGAN. So that, in itself, is a gift."

JOANNA AMPIL
Award-winning singer/actress

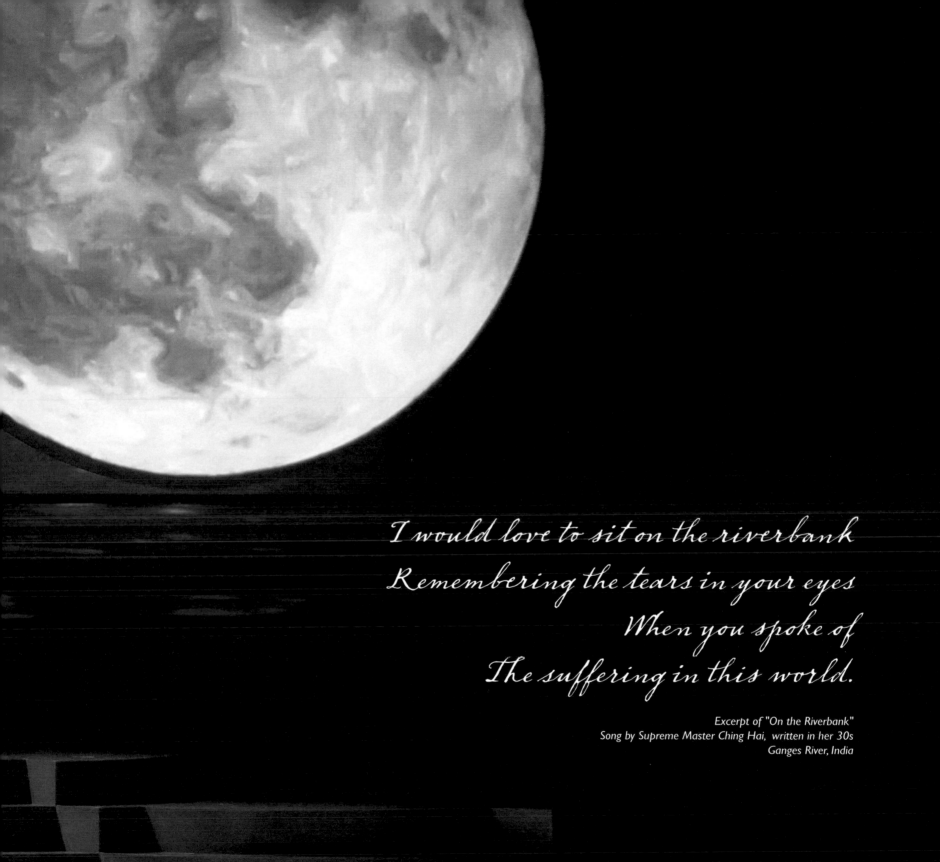

I would love to sit on the riverbank
Remembering the tears in your eyes
When you spoke of
The suffering in this world.

Excerpt of "On the Riverbank"
Song by Supreme Master Ching Hai, written in her 30s
Ganges River, India

SCENE SEVEN
MUD HOUSE IN RISHIKESH

Three or four days later. KLAUS is relaxing in the sun. He is reading a religious text and munching a carrot.

KLAUS: India's hot! "To become one with the planet, one must become a tree." Who's one?

(Losing interest in the carrot, he tosses it aside. He picks up a tattered copy of MAD Magazine.)

KLAUS: Oh, I get it. When you fold it, its chin becomes a butt. Hahaha, that's funny.

(THANH approaches from offstage. KLAUS quickly, guiltily, disposes of the magazine. But it is too late – she has seen him.)

THANH: *(laughing)* Guilty pleasures!

KLAUS: No, no, no, no, no… This isn't mine. Oh, Thanh.

THANH: Klaus, your secret is safe with me! Go gently with yourself, my gentle friend! And look! *(She holds up a bag of flour.)* Flour from the market for homemade chapattis!

KLAUS: *(unenthusiastically)* Delicious. So, Thanh – how are you sleeping these days? Up there on the roof…!

THANH: My five-zillion star hotel? I sleep like a lamb in a pasture.

KLAUS: Still, all in all, it can't be very safe. You know, the scorpions everywhere! And it rains. A lot. And there's room, you know, inside this mud house…

THANH: Where? In that tiny cot?

KLAUS: Yeah!

THANH: Klaus…

KLAUS: Oh no, no, I'll sleep on the floor. With a mat. And a blanket.

THANH: Klaus. How can I make you understand what I mean

when I say – I absolutely ADORE you…AND I'm going to keep sleeping on the roof. *(A beat, in which KLAUS looks forlorn.)* In any case – it will soon be time for me to be pressing on.

KLAUS: Why do you have to press on? It's beautiful here. We're eating well, growing wiser every day just living, just being…aren't we?

THANH: You know, the woman who gave me her walking stick, she called me Smiling Step. She knew, I think, that my journey would be long but joyful. There's this inner joy within me that wants to keep going forward. If I am to find a true Master I have to climb higher into the Himalayas.

KLAUS: "Smiling Step"…

THANH: *(smiling broadly)* Yes. *(A beat.)* But meanwhile, I have to finish shopping! So, if you're hungry, have some sprouts. *(She hands him a container from the market.)*

KLAUS: *(half-heartedly)* Oh I will, I love these.

(THANH leaves. KLAUS stares after her, totally lovesick. Then he looks at the sprouts. He munches a few. He picks up another book – it is a notebook of THANH's. He guiltily opens to a page at random.)

KLAUS: Oh Thanh, you forgot your book… *(reading)* "If there

wasn't you in life/Where would I have run?/Maybe to a monastery". *(He shuts the book. Music begins.)* I can do better than that!

"IF IT WASN'T FOR SPROUTS IN LIFE"

KLAUS:
IF IT WASN'T FOR SPROUTS IN LIFE
I WOULD HAVE GONE TO THE MOON,
SITTING THERE MISERABLE
LIKE A DOG WITHOUT BONES!

IF IT WASN'T FOR SPROUTS IN LIFE
I WOULD HAVE BEEN SO LONESOME;
THINK OF THE SUNFLOWER
WITHOUT THE SHINING SUN!

IF IT WASN'T FOR SPROUTS IN LIFE
OH WHERE TO WOULD I HAVE RUN?
MAYBE TO A MONASTERY
BUT THERE I MUST BE SO LONELY
LIKE A MONK WITHOUT A NUN!

(KLAUS is joined by assorted tap dancing FARMERS from the local fields.)

IF IT WASN'T FOR SPROUTS IN LIFE
OH WHERE TO WOULD I HAVE RUN?
MAYBE TO A MONASTERY
BUT THERE I MUST BE SO LONELY
LIKE A MONK WITHOUT A NUN!

(At the end of the number, FARMERS exit and ROLF appears, dusty and disheveled.)

KLAUS: *(shocked)* Dr. Reinhardt!!

ROLF: *(quietly)* Hallo, Klaus.

KLAUS: Where did you – !? How did you – !?!

ROLF: Find you? The usual way – an airplane, a bus, a water buffalo, my own two legs. I travel equipped with three things that have proven sufficient: my passport, a handful of traveler's cheques, and this letter that you sent to Elsa. *(He removes it from his shirt pocket and holds it up for KLAUS to see.)*

KLAUS: *(utterly confused)* Oh...?

ROLF: Did you not think that she would show it to me?

KLAUS: Well…

ROLF: And did you not think that I would make note of the return address which you so dutifully scrawled on the envelope? But you weren't there. I showed her picture at every ashram, bank and post office between here and Delhi.

KLAUS: Oh...?

ROLF: Where is she?

KLAUS: Who?

ROLF: My wife.

KLAUS: *(A beat. He finally gets what's going on.)* She's not here. She's out gathering food for our supper.

ROLF: So she does live here.

KLAUS: *(with a growing defiance)* Yes.

ROLF: With you?

KLAUS: Yes!

ROLF: With you!?!

KLAUS: YES!!! We – we're both on the same spiritual path, you know. We met – I helped her, saved her, actually, from a particularly dangerous situation. And she was very grateful!

ROLF: Go on.

KLAUS: And I think – no, I know – she does not want to go back to Germany with you, Doctor, if that is what you are assuming.

ROLF: That is none of your business.

🌹 The Real Love

KLAUS: No, no, it is my business. Because I'm in love with her!

ROLF: And she...you!?

KLAUS: Yes. She adores me. She told me so.

ROLF: (A beat. Then, quietly, urgently, almost to himself) I don't believe it! It's like a bad dream! What a fool I've been! To have gone on this exhausting, idiotic, wild goose chase! Do me a favor, Klaus. Tell Thanh I was here. Show this to her! – (He puts the letter on the box.) It will prove what inspired my visit! I'll be back in Munich. (ROLF exits.)

KLAUS: Oh Klaus… (KLAUS, shaking and dazed, sits with his head in his hands. THANH reappears with a basket of food.)

THANH: I'm back!

KLAUS: (startled) Oh, so quickly! Hi! (She unpacks her basket.)

THANH: Hey, what's this? Your letter to Elsa from Germany? How did this get here?

KLAUS: Rolf brought it.

THANH: Rolf? Here!? When??

KLAUS: Just now.

THANH: (thrilled) Wh – ! Well, where is he?

KLAUS: He left. I sent him away.

THANH: What??

KLAUS: Okay, he left. He was pretty angry.

THANH: But why??

KLAUS: Because we are living together.

THANH: But that's ridiculous! Did you tell him the truth? That I sleep on the roof!? And you're here temporarily until you find your own hut!

KLAUS: I told him the truth… I told him I was in love with you,

Thanh.

THANH: (A beat.) Oh, Klaus. You great, big idiot.

KLAUS: I know.

THANH: Why did you do such a thing?

KLAUS: Because it's the truth! Because it's, it's pure, it's real! And because – because I was afraid. I was afraid that if I didn't tell him I was in love with you, he was going to take you away, and I would never see you again.

THANH: (A beat. Quietly) Klaus. Didn't I just tell you I absolutely adore you? But Rolf is my husband. And I am IN LOVE with him.

KLAUS: I see. I see that.

THANH: Which way did he go, Klaus?

KLAUS: That way. (He points in the opposite direction from where ROLF has just left. THANH races to gather her things. She starts off in the direction he has pointed.) No, wait...that way. (He points in the correct direction. She exits.)

(Lights fade on KLAUS – forlorn and miserable.)

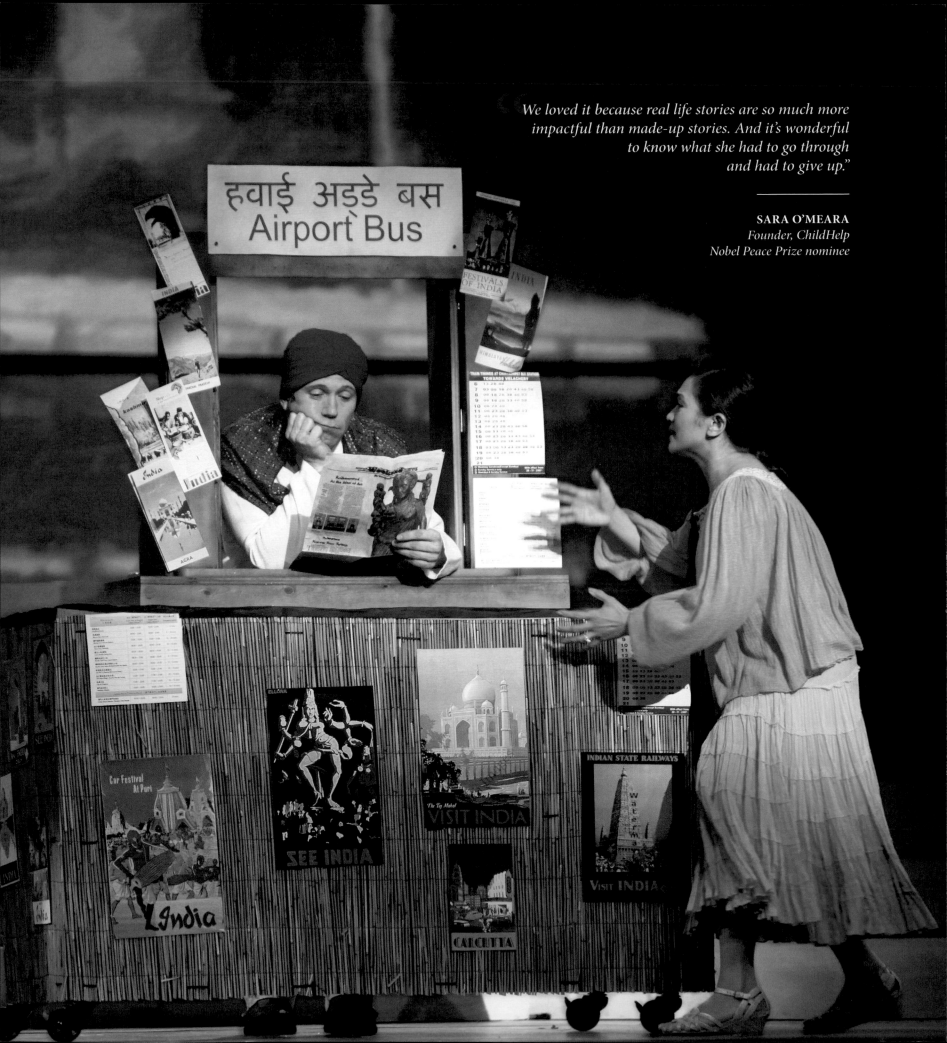

We loved it because real life stories are so much more impactful than made-up stories. And it's wonderful to know what she had to go through and had to give up."

SARA O'MEARA
Founder, ChildHelp
Nobel Peace Prize nominee

SCENE EIGHT
STREETS OF RISHIKESH

THANH is seen racing into the teeming city, seeking ROLF. Music throughout. Citizens from all walks of life are going about their business.

THANH: *(to a MERCHANT)* Excuse me, did a tall, German man, Westerner pass this way?

MERCHANT: Straight ahead!

THANH: Thank you.

(More movement. She asks the same question, again and again, in pantomime. The responses vary from dismissal, to apologetic confusion, to the ubiquitous "Straight ahead!")

THANH: *(to a TRAFFIC COP, shouting over traffic noise)* Excuse me! Could you show me the directions to the bus depot?

COP: Straight ahead!

THANH: That's impossible!

COP: Follow the traffic circle two quarters round, make a hard left at the hotel, and go two more blocks.

THANH: Bless you!

COP: Can't miss it.

(More music, movement, chaos and confusion. We lose sight of THANH.)

(Crossfade to the bus depot. ROLF is buying a ticket at a window.)

ROLF: *(to TICKET SELLER)* One ticket to the airport, please.

(The transaction complete, he turns to go to his bus.)

(THANH enters the bus depot breathlessly, just in time to see ROLF disappear through the gate. Sound of the bus pulling out.)

THANH: Rolf! Rolf! *(THANH rushes to the ticket window.)* That

bus! Stop that bus!

TICKET SELLER: Too late.

THANH: But a man got on it! I need to talk to him!

TICKET SELLER: Too late. On the way to the airport. On time.

THANH: Airport?! I need to catch him. Please.

TICKET SELLER: Sorry, miss. Too late. That was the last one today. *(He slams the window shut.)*

THANH: I missed him. I just missed him. *(sinking slowly to the ground)* He must have been so angry with me. And for no good reason. A silly, foolish misunderstanding. And I didn't get a chance to...explain. Or to tell him how much I love him. Oh, Rolf. *(She cries.)*

SCENE NINE
MUD HOUSE

THANH sitting motionless, still saddened by ROLF's departure.

KLAUS: (brings THANH a bowl of food) Thanh… Thanh, it's been days. Eat something, you've got to eat. *(THANH remains unresponsive.)* Thanh, I'm sorry, but face it. He would've already received your telegrams in Munich by now. Rolf's not coming back. You've got to move on.

THANH: Move on?

KLAUS: Yes. Stay here! With me! I'll take care of you, Thanh.

THANH: No. I need to be alone. To think. And to pray. I'm going away.

KLAUS: Where? When?

THANH: I'm going up the Himalayas. I'm leaving now.

KLAUS: Let me come with you.

THANH: Klaus. No. Thank you. But...no. Goodbye. *(She swiftly gathers her traveling gear and exits. KLAUS is left, as usual, forlorn and bereft.)*

SCENE TEN
HALFWAY UP THE PATH TO GANGOTRI

THANH is at a makeshift fruit cart.

THANH: (to the FRUIT VENDOR) Namaste, am I anywhere close to Gangotri?

FRUIT VENDOR: I am sorry, but not really. Still very far. And miss, it is not the custom of our country for a woman to travel alone. It can be very dangerous. But we have very nice mangoes!

(ROLF has come up from behind THANH, unseen. He puts his hands over her eyes. She is startled and struggles to free herself.)

ROLF: He is right. A woman should never travel alone. She should always bring along her husband, whenever possible.

THANH: (turns to face him) ROLF!

(They embrace.)

ROLF: Happy birthday, darling.

THANH: Happy birthday.

ROLF: I never left India. Something stopped me. It was you. I needed to see you. I've been searching for you for two days. I realized what a fool I've been. Still am. A fool in love, Thanh.

THANH: You can be a very silly man, Dr. Reinhardt.

ROLF: I just needed to see you. To hold you. I've been completely miserable without you, Thanh. It's as simple as that.

THANH: You sweet, adorable man. What now?

ROLF: I don't care. Just as long as we're together.

THANH: But your work! The new children's wing. You've been dreaming of that for years.

ROLF: Yes, it opens the day after tomorrow.

THANH: You would love to be there.

ROLF: No! It couldn't be less important to me now, Thanh. My life's work is loving you. Lead on, and I will follow.

THANH: But you're a doctor.

ROLF: *(laughing)* Well, of course, I'm a doctor. I'm also a dentist, remember?

THANH: I mean, it's your life, your passion, your calling.

ROLF: I'm on a different path, now, Thanh.

THANH: This is my path, Rolf.

ROLF: Yes. So what do we do now?

THANH: Carry on.

ROLF: How? Where?

THANH: I'm continuing my journey...up the Himalayas. *(She points towards the far-off mountains.)* And you... You

 **The Real Love**

"The last duet ('Our Time'), it just brought chills down my spine, it's just so powerful. With great lyrics and a great composition, it's very beautiful.

Through all of the hatred that we have in this world and all of the wars and the suffering, the fact that Supreme Master Ching Hai can still find a path of happiness, enlightenment, is just so inspiring. Especially as an artist, it's something that I'll certainly keep with me for quite some time."

DOMINIC PACE
Award-winning actor

are going back to Munich.

ROLF: So, you couldn't...come with me?

THANH: *(fighting tears)* No, my love. We both know this is just...the truth.

ROLF: When will I see you again?

THANH: Someday. I hope.

ROLF: I will love you always and forever, Thanh.

THANH: And I will love you – forever and always.

"OUR TIME"

THANH:
THE TIME WE SPEND TOGETHER
I WILL ALWAYS TREASURE
DO NOT FORGET OUR MEMORY
FOR LOVE IS THE ONE AND ONLY.

ROLF:
WHO SAYS THE WORLD IS EPHEMERAL?
IF WE ARE TOGETHER IT'S ETERNAL.
DREAM AND LIFE MERGE IN UNISON
WHEN OUR SOULS ARE ONE.

THANH:
THE PEACE WITHIN IS THE PEACE WITHOUT
HEAVEN WILL BE HERE AND NOW!

ROLF:
FOR THOSE WHO FOUND TRUE LOVE
FLOWERS OF EDEN BLOOM IN THEIR SOULS.

THANH:
WE LIVE IN GOD, WE LIVE IN MEN,

ROLF:
WE LIVE IN HAPPINESS THAT NEVER ENDS.

THANH:
WE WALK IN BEAUTY, WE WALK IN BLISS

ROLF:
WE LAUGH, WE SING TO OUR HEART'S CONTENT.

THANH:
FORGET ME NOT,

ROLF:
FORGET US NOT

BOTH:
FOR US IS ALL THAT WE HAVE GOT.
WHAT ELSE IS THERE FOR ONE TO HOLD
TO FILL THE EMPTINESS IN OUR SOULS?

THANH:
THE LOVE WE SHARE IS THE LOVE WE SAVE,
LOVE FROM HEAVEN ON EARTH DESCENDS.

BOTH:
THE LOVE IN YOU, THE LOVE IN ME
IS THE LOVE OF GOD THAT EVER BE!

(They each turn away and exit in opposite directions.)

"The Real Love *gave the message of world peace and just to be happy and to love each other. As soon as I heard about this project, I immediately wanted to participate in it because I think it has such a good message for the world.*"

KIRIL KULISH
Tony Award-winning actor/dancer/singer

SCENE ELEVEN
GANGOTRI

PILGRIMS gather around the intense blue waters of Gangotri, the source of the Ganges River.

PILGRIMS:
STOP! LOOK!
LOOK, GANGOTRI!
THE SOURCE OF THE GANGES!
MOTHER GANGES, GANGA MA!
MOTHER GANGES, GANGA MA!
MOTHER GANGES, GANGA MA!

(THANH enters, wearing a blue sari. A PILGRIM takes a corner of her sari and unwraps it. It is passed from hand to hand amongst the PILGRIMS, who unwrap THANH as they continue to encircle her, with the blue cloth representing the Ganges River.)

SPLASH THE WATER ON YOUR FACE!
DIP YOUR HANDS!
PLUNGE YOUR FEET!
PLUNGE YOUR FACE AND HANDS AND FEET –
LET ALL YOUR SINS BE CLEANSED!

(THANH emerges from the river, dressed in a simple white tunic. She moves upwards toward the high peaks of the Himalayas, alone, leaving the PILGRIMS.)

(One by one, ELSA, KLAUS, GRETA, RAJEEV, YOUNG THANH, LINH and ROLF appear and join the PILGRIMS.)

"THE PEACE SEEKER"

ELSA:
ONCE UPON A TIME,
A TRUE PEACE LOVER
WANDERED AROUND THE MANY WORLDS
IN SEARCH OF ETERNAL HAPPINESS.
SHE WALKED OVER THE FACE OF THE EARTH,
THE SUNS, THE MOONS AND THE CLOUDS.

PILGRIMS:
AT LAST SHE FOUND:
THAT IT WAS ALL THE WHILE
HIDDEN IN HER VERY HEART.

KLAUS:
THEN SHE SAT DOWN
AND WAS ABOUT TO ENJOY THE NEWFOUND BLISS.

ELSA, KLAUS and PILGRIMS:
BUT SUDDENLY SHE LOOKED DOWN:
AND SAW COUNTLESS BEINGS WERE STILL
GROVELING IN DARKNESS,

GRETA:
FOR THEY WERE SEARCHING FOR HAPPINESS
WITHOUT,
JUST LIKE HER BEFORE, ERRING OVER MILLIONS OF
AGES.

GRETA and PILGRIMS:
HER TEARS WERE THEN ROLLING DOWN...

LINH:
ONE DROP

RAJEEV and YOUNG THANH:
TWO DROPS...

ALL:
AND MANY MORE...
EACH DROP BECAME A SHINING JEWEL

ROLF:
AND SOON THE FIRMAMENT WAS STUDDED WITH
GLITTERING TEARS

ALL:
WHICH ARE THE STARS TODAY;
THEY ARE TOO SHY IN THE DAY
AND TOO RESTLESS IN THE NIGHT
TO GO TO SLEEP.
FOR ALL PEACE SEEKERS,
THE STARS ARE THERE TO LIGHT THE WAY
ETERNAL HAPPINESS, ETERNAL PEACE.
ETERNAL HAPPINESS AND PEACE.

(THANH, finally reaching the highest possible point on the set, turns upstage, raises her arms in a gesture of discovery and triumph. A blazing, almost blinding white light envelops her.)

(Curtain.)

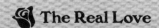 The Real Love

Each drop became a shining Jewel
and soon the firmament was studded with glittering tears
which are the stars today;

For all peace seekers,
The stars are there to light the Way

Excerpts of "The Peace Seeker"
Poem by Supreme Master Ching Hai, written in her early 30s

PHOTO MEMORIES *(Supreme Master Ching Hai with her former husband Dr. Dr. Rolf G.)*

Schwarzwald, Germany ~ 1979

Rapallo, Italy ~ early 1980s

Rapallo, Italy ~ early 1980s

Rapallo, Italy ~ early 1980s

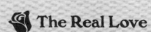 The Real Love

Germany ~ early 1980s

Munich, Germany ~ early 1980s

Germany ~ early 1980s

Pilgrimage in Thailand ~ early 1980s

BIOGRAPHIES

Supreme Master Ching Hai (Vegan)
France - August 15, 2009

Supreme Master Ching Hai

Supreme Master Ching Hai is a world-renowned spiritual teacher, humanitarian, author, poet and artist, who envisions a world of love, beauty and kindness for all.

Born in central Âu Lạc (Vietnam), Supreme Master Ching Hai studied in Europe and worked there for the Red Cross. She soon found that suffering exists in all corners of the globe, and finding a remedy to this became the foremost goal in her life.

She was happily married at the time to a German physician, and although it was an extremely difficult decision for both of them, her husband agreed to a separation. She then embarked on a journey alone in search of spiritual enlightenment. In the remote Himalayas in India, finally she received from a true Master the divine transmission of the inner Light and Sound, which she later called the Quan Yin Method of meditation. After a period of diligent practice, she attained the Great Enlightenment.

Soon after her return from the Himalayas, at the earnest requests of those who came to her, Supreme Master Ching Hai shared the Quan Yin Method so that others too may rediscover their true great Self and source of happiness. She has been invited to give numerous lectures by world governments and esteemed organizations.

Supreme Master Ching Hai donates the proceeds from her creative works to many charitable projects around the world to help humans in need and protect our vulnerable animal friends as well as the environment. She is also the guiding inspiration for the global channel Supreme Master Television and its all-constructive programming for a more peaceful world.

The innumerable honors recognizing her selfless service and artistic contributions include the Award for Promotion of Human Rights, 2002 Los Angeles Music Week Certificate of Commendation, 2006 Gusi Peace Prize, First Place Silver for the 27th Annual Telly Awards, 2008 US Presidential Active Lifestyle Award and 2010 US President's Volunteer Service Award.

Supreme Master Ching Hai's care for all co-inhabitants of the Earth continues to touch and uplift countless lives. She leads a vegan lifestyle that reflects her compassionate heart and eco-friendly values.

> *"The biologist and the artist and art lover all have a love for life inside, deep inside, and we all have the capacity of sensitivity that artists or scientists possess. We just have to kindle and cultivate these qualities. So we all do what we can to spread positive, happy consciousness within our world, to lessen sorrow and suffering, to bring love and peace into our lives and the lives of all on this planet."*
>
> *Supreme Master Ching Hai*
> *Thailand - May 29, 2011*

"A beautiful story full of love and consciousness of the universe."

LYNNE WINTERSTELLER
Soprano

"I'm bowled over by the talent that they have here, all the Grammys and Academy Awards and Emmys connected to the names that got involved in this production. I think everything that I see the Supreme Master Ching Hai is doing is for peace and love; anywhere you can find it, you spread it to all living things."

GRANT ALEKSANDER (Vegetarian)
Four-time Emmy Award-nominated actor

"I just respect Supreme Master Ching Hai so much for her whole thought and the wonderful things she does for animals. I think she's giving of herself and that's so nice to see. It's so generous, and I appreciate her very much."

DICK VAN PATTEN
Actor (Eight Is Enough)

"I spent years working at Radio City, which is a pretty big venue for shows, 6,000 people it seats, but I've never experienced anything of the size of The Real Love with such a short amount of time."

DON PIPPIN
Tony & Emmy Award-winning composer & music director

"Usually I am on stage, so I am absolutely thrilled to be in the audience and hear this wonderful music."

FLORENCE LARUE
Grammy Award-winning singer

The Real Love

COMPOSERS

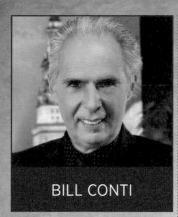

BILL CONTI

ACADEMY & 5-TIME EMMY AWARD WINNER

Bill Conti is one of Hollywood's most prominent film and television composers and conductors. He won the Academy Award for Best Original Score for *The Right Stuff* (1983) and two Oscar nominations for Best Original Song: one for "Gonna Fly Now" from the 1976 blockbuster film *Rocky*, and one for the theme song of the James Bond film *For Your Eyes Only* (1981), performed by Sheena Easton.

A graduate of the Julliard School of Music, Mr. Conti has composed for over 70 diverse feature films, including *The Karate Kid* movies, *The Thomas Crown Affair* and *The Adventures of Huck Finn*. His prolific works include recognizable themes for television such as *Good Morning America*, *The Lifestyles of the Rich and Famous*, *ABC Sports* and *Inside Edition*. He has been recognized with five Emmy Awards for his work in television.

Mr. Conti served as music director for the internationally live-broadcast Academy Awards ceremony an amazing 19 times. A sought-after conductor of the world's most prestigious orchestras, he was also music director for the 4th of July gala at Ford's Theatre in Washington, DC with US President Barack Obama.

Among Mr. Conti's many accolades is a star bearing his name on the Hollywood Walk of Fame.

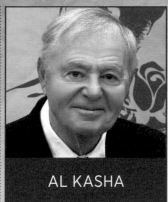

AL KASHA

2-TIME ACADEMY AWARD WINNER

Al Kasha is a gifted composer and brilliant lyricist who has made hit records over an illustrious five decades, with works sung by artists such as Elvis Presley, Aretha Franklin and Donna Summer.

His songs, "The Morning After" from the *The Poseidon Adventure* and "We May Never Love Like This Again" from *The Towering Inferno*, each won an Academy Award for Best Song. Mr. Kasha created these plus many more acclaimed scores, including for Walt Disney's beloved classic *Pete's Dragon*, which garnered two Oscar nominations. Also to Mr. Kasha's credit are the animated classic *All Dogs Go to Heaven* (Fennecus Award for Best Song/Score), the Golden Globe-nominated Disney film *Freaky Friday* and *Rudolph, the Red-Nosed Reindeer* starring John Goodman and Whoopi Goldberg.

In theater, Mr. Kasha received two Tony Award nominations, one for Best Original Score for his work on *Seven Brides for Seven Brothers*, and another for *Copperfield*, the Broadway musical based on Charles Dickens' classic.

Also recognized with two Grammy Award nominations, four Golden Globe nominations, and the People's Choice Award, Mr. Kasha accepted the MovieGuide Awards' Lifetime Achievement Award in February 2011.

DOUG KATSAROS

EMMY AWARD NOMINEE

Doug Katsaros is a dedicated composer, arranger, orchestrator, vocalist, conductor and keyboardist. He has worked with Donny Osmond, Rod Stewart, Gloria Estefan, Sir Elton John, Bon Jovi, Frank Sinatra, Peter Paul & Mary and Cher, among others.

For theater, Mr. Katsaros composed, arranged, conducted and/or orchestrated for a host of Broadway and Off-Broadway productions such as *Laughing Room Only*, *The Life*, *Footloose*, *The Rocky Horror Show*, *Diamonds*, the Outer Critics Circle Award-winning *A… My Name Is Alice* and *The Toxic Avenger*. For his contribution to Off-Broadway's *Altar Boyz*, he was nominated for the Drama Desk Award for Outstanding Orchestrations.

His work on the popular animated series *The Tick*, *Macuso FBI*, and ABC's *Afterschool Specials* garnered Emmy Award nominations for Outstanding Music Composition.

Other compositions and performances on television include *The Jim Henson Hour*, *Larry King Live*, "By Mennen" jingle and films such as *If Lucy Fell* with Sarah Jessica Parker and *Me and the Mob* starring Sandra Bullock.

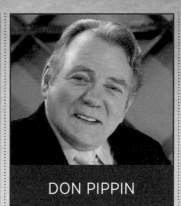

DON PIPPIN

TONY & EMMY AWARD WINNER

One of Broadway's most esteemed musical directors as well as composers, Donald Pippin has contributed to productions including *Cabaret*, *Mack and Mabel*, *Mame* and *La Cage aux Folles*. He won a Tony Award for *Oliver!*, an Emmy Award for *Broadway Sings: The Music of Jule Styne*, a Drama Desk Award for his contribution to theater, and a gold record for *A Chorus Line*.

He served 12 years as music director of New York's famed Radio City Music Hall. In addition, he has been a guest conductor of the famed Boston Pops Orchestra, Los Angeles and New York Philharmonic orchestras, and UK's Royal Philharmonic Orchestra, among others. Mr. Pippin was a music director for "An Evening with Alan Jay Lerner", the gala for the 100th birthday of Cole Porter at Carnegie Hall and London's Prince Edward Theatre, and "Jerry Herman's Broadway", a star-studded Hollywood Bowl television special. He toured with Marilyn Horne, including her performance at President Bill Clinton's inauguration.

As a classically trained pianist, Mr. Pippin has accompanied great entertainers such as Peggy Lee, Frank Sinatra, Angela Lansbury, Julie Andrews and Tony Bennett.

Along with his kind wife, Mr. Pippin enjoys spending time with his adopted animal companions.

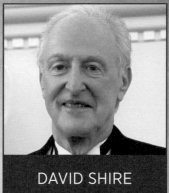

DAVID SHIRE

ACADEMY & 2-TIME GRAMMY AWARD WINNER

David Shire received the Academy Award for the song "It Goes Like It Goes" from *Norma Rae* and two Grammy Awards for his original music for *Saturday Night Fever*. Among his numerous feature film scores are those for *The Conversation*, *The Taking of Pelham 1-2-3*, *All the President's Men* and *Zodiac*. His songs have been performed and recorded by the likes of Barbra Streisand, Melissa Manchester, Vanessa Williams, Jennifer Warnes and Julie Andrews, to name just a few.

For Broadway, Mr. Shire has composed the music for the musicals *Baby* and *Big*, both of which garnered Tony nominations for Best Score. Off-Broadway shows include the Grammy-nominated *Starting Here, Starting Now* and *Closer Than Ever*, which won the Outer Critics Circle Award.

His numerous television scores have earned five Emmy nominations, and include *Sarah, Plain and Tall* starring Glenn Close, *Rear Window* with Christopher Reeve, *Raid on Entebbe*, and *The Women of Brewster Place* produced by Oprah Winfrey.

With his talented wife, actress Didi Conn (*Grease*), Mr. Shire is co-developing the children's musical television series *Didi Lightful*. He is a Society of Composers and Lyricists Ambassador and serves on the Dramatists Guild of America's executive council.

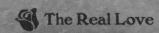

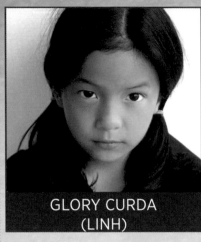

**JOANNA AMPIL
(THANH)**

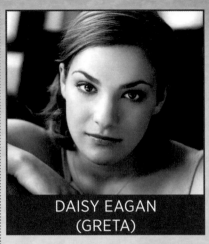

**GLORY CURDA
(LINH)**

**DAISY EAGAN
(GRETA)**

TONY AWARD WINNER

**CADY HUFFMAN
(ELSA)**

TONY AWARD WINNER

Award-winning international theater actress Joanna Ampil has been a sensation in London's West End as well as her native Philippines. She has collaborated with Lord Andrew Lloyd Webber, Claude-Michel Schönberg and Jason Robert Brown, to name a few. She starred as Kim in *Miss Saigon*, and performed in many other musicals including *Jesus Christ Superstar*, *Les Misérables*, *Rent* and *Avenue Q*.

Glory Curda had her professional theater debut as Ballon Girl in *Gypsy* with the West Coast Ensemble. Recent television appearances include *Law & Order: SVU* (NBC) and *Make It or Break It* (ABC Family). Her most recent film credit is her lead role of Nellie in *Pocketful of Posey*.

Daisy Eagan became the youngest female ever to win a Tony Award for her performance as Mary Lennox in *The Secret Garden*. Her other theater credits include *Les Misérables*, *James Joyce's The Dead*, and *The Wild Party* (LA Weekly Award for Best Supporting Actress in a Musical). Her film and TV appearances include *Losing Isaiah*, *Without a Trace*, *Ghost Whisperer* and *Numb3rs*.

Cady Huffman is perhaps best known on Broadway for her Tony Award-winning performance as Ulla in *The Producers*. In feature films, Cady has been in *The Company Men* opposite Ben Affleck and Chris Cooper, and *Hero* with Dustin Hoffman, Geena Davis and Andy Garcia. Her television credits include appearances on *Curb Your Enthusiasm*, *Mad About You* and *Frasier*, among many others.

BETTY BUCKLEY

TONY AWARD WINNER

FILIPPA GIORDANO

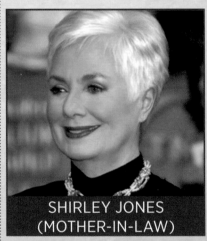

**SHIRLEY JONES
(MOTHER-IN-LAW)**

ACADEMY AWARD WINNER

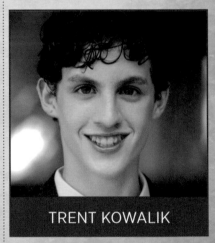

TRENT KOWALIK

TONY AWARD WINNER

The acclaimed Betty Buckley received the Tony Award for her performance as Grizabella in the original cast of *Cats*. She played Hesione in *Triumph of Love* (Tony nomination) and Norma Desmond in *Sunset Boulevard* (Olivier Award nomination). She has received two Grammy nominations for her recordings. Ms. Buckley also starred in the television series *Eight Is Enough* and has appeared in films such as *Carrie*, *Tender Mercies* and *The Happening*.

Award-winning Italian singer Filippa Giordano's albums have topped world classical charts and reached gold status. She has sung with ABBA's Frida and Oscar winner Vangelis, and performed for Pope John Paul II and the Academy Awards. In 2000, HRH Prince Charles of Wales invited Filippa to hold a concert and New York City Mayor Michael Bloomberg hosted a dinner in her honor.

Oscar winner and 3-time Emmy nominee Shirley Jones was nicknamed America's Cinderella Sweetheart for her wholesome roles in musical films such as *Carousel*, *Oklahoma!* and *The Music Man*. She won the Academy Award for Best Supporting Actress in 1960 for her performance in *Elmer Gantry*. She is also well-known for playing the matriarch in *The Partridge Family* television series.

Tony-winning actor, dancer and singer Trent Kowalik made his theatrical debut as Billy in *Billy Elliot the Musical*, with music by Sir Elton John and book and lyrics by Lee Hall. He earned the Tony Award for Best Actor in a Musical, as well as the Fred Astaire Award, Theatre World Award and Outer Critics Circle Special Achievement Award.

 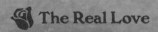

MUEEN JAHAN
(RAJEEV/SADHU)

Mueen Jahan, who holds a Master of Fine Arts degree, has performed in notable theatrical works such as *Bombay Dreams, Homebody/Kabul, Galileo, Suburbia, Snow Queen, Asylum* (LA Ovation Award nomination) and *Much Ado About Nothing.* Television and film work include *An American Carol, Victorious, The Sopranos, Law & Order* and *The Tonight Show with Jay Leno.*

ADAM PASCAL
(ROLF)

TONY AWARD NOMINEE

Adam Pascal garnered a Tony Award nomination for his role as Roger Davis in the original US and UK casts of *Rent*, the musical. He went on to star in the film *Rent*. Also on Broadway, he has performed in *Aida* as the lead and in *Cabaret* as the MC. Adam is currently in the band Me and Larry, with Larry Edoff.

ROBERT TORTI
(KLAUS)

TONY AWARD NOMINEE

Robert Torti is well remembered for playing Greaseball in *Starlight Express*, for which he was nominated for a Tony Award. His other theater credits include *Godspell* (Drama-Logue Award), *West Side Story* and *Grease*. Robert's many television and film productions include *The Drew Carey Show, Beverly Hills 90210* and *Family Ties*. He was in the musical movie *That Thing You Do!*, which garnered him a gold record.

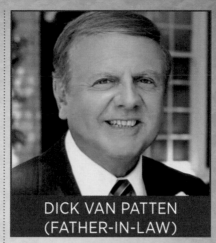

DICK VAN PATTEN
(FATHER-IN-LAW)

Best known as the patriarch Tom Bradford on the hit sitcom *Eight Is Enough*, the prolific Dick Van Patten has been in 27 Broadway plays, 600 radio shows, and dozens of feature films and television series. Mr. Van Patten has a star on the Hollywood Walk of Fame and is the author of several bestselling books. His newest book, a memoir, is titled *Eighty Is Not Enough*.

KIRIL KULISH

TONY AWARD WINNER

Kiril Kulish is a Tony-winning actor, dancer, singer and musician. He is best known for playing Billy in Sir Elton John and Lee Hall's *Billy Elliot the Musical* for which he won the Tony Award for Best Actor in a Musical. He was also honored with a Fred Astaire Award, Theatre World Award and Outer Critics Circle Special Achievement Award.

FAITH RIVERA

EMMY AWARD WINNER

The inspirational music of Faith Rivera has been featured on popular television shows including *ER, Scrubs* and *Passions*. Faith received an Emmy Award in 2003 for Outstanding Original Song with "Forever Near". She has released six solo CDs and has collaborated with 7 time Grammy winner Al Jarreau and acclaimed artist Brian McKnight in recording the song "Give Your Love" to promote peace.

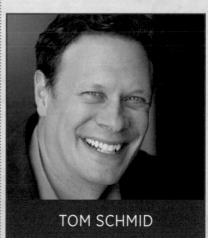

TOM SCHMID

Praised for his rich tenor voice, Tom Schmid has an impressive list of theater, film and television credits. He has performed on Broadway and played the star dual roles in *Jekyll & Hyde*, Raoul in *The Phantom of the Opera* and Captain von Trapp in *The Sound of Music*. Tom has been seen on *Desperate Housewives, CSI: Miami, Bones, Charmed, Gilmore Girls* and more.

LYNNE WINTERSTELLER

Lynne Wintersteller, a soprano and actress, has appeared in the Off-Broadway hit *Closer Than Ever*, for which she was nominated for a Drama Desk Award for Best Actress in a Musical. Her other credits include *A Grand Night for Singing, Annie, Company, Richard Cory* (New York Musical Theatre Festival's Best Actress Award) and *The Ghost & Mrs. Muir* (Los Angeles Ovation nomination).

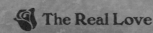

Sheet Music & Poems

It's very nice because the lyrics that Supreme Master wrote are very special and so true. It's such a strong energy there. It's a very peaceful and creative and fresh atmosphere."

FILIPPA GIORDIANO
Italian singer

THE REAL LOVE

Lyrics based on
Supreme Master Ching Hai's
poem written in April 2011

Music by Don Pippin

The Real Love

THE REAL LOVE

Let's make life more simp - le, let our de - mands be lit - tle.

Then you'll know hap - pi - ness e - ver more and more!____

Then we don't have to go on snatch - ing land.____

Nor have we to hur-ry on con-vert-ing man.

It's not how ma-ny in a be-lief sys-tem,

it's what be-comes of them!

it's what be-comes of them! It's

It's not our words, it's ra-ther loud-er our ac-tions. What is

It's not our words, it's ra-ther loud-er our ac-tions. What is

go-ing to be our le-gend in the long his-tory of hu-mans? Will it be

go-ing to be our le-gend in the long his-tory of hu-mans?

right and just Will it be nob-le and be - ne-vo-lent? Or just a grim pic-ture

While our sur-vi-val is the cost of oth-ers' ex-tinc-tion!

Wood Block

What is the mark of the "cho-sen"? Is it just the blood-stain on your hands?

Be it from a-ni-mals or man's! Oh my

Hea - ven on Earth? The

Hea - ven on Earth? The

Real Love!

Real Love!

WHAT CAN I DO WITH MY HEART

Lyrics based on Supreme Master Ching Hai's
poem written in September 1978
Munich, Germany

Thanh

from *The Real Love*
Music by Don Pippin

WHAT CAN I DO WITH MY HEART

WHAT CAN I DO WITH MY HEART

Freely

Cannot Do a Thing with My Heart

By Supreme Master Ching Hai in her late 20s
Originally in English

I want to throw away my heart,
It hurts me so much daily,
With every misfortune, with everyone!
In the world full of misery!

This expensive thing I possess,
That I could never sell, nor throw away!
This little heart of mine!
So little and so fine
Beats enormously
With the world full of misery!

I am going to the Wizard of Oz,
Let him take my heart away!

Won't be hurt anymore,
With the world today.
What can I do with my heart?
What can I do with her?
It hurts me every day;
It hurts me every night!
What can I do for the world?
What can I do for my people?
Always full of troubles,
Always full of sorrow!

My ears listen to musique,
My eyes adore beauty,
My lips sing poetry.
But my heart is full of melancholy!
She wouldn't let me free.

If there is reincarnation,
I am going to be a flower,
A fruit, a tree or a plant.
But never, never,
A human being again!

Munich, Germany - September 1978
From the poetry collection:
The Dream of a Butterfly

Lyrics based on Supreme Master Ching Hai's
poem written in Spring 1979
Munich, Germany

Thanh & Company

from *The Real Love*
Music by Al Kasha

The Real Love

Yearning for Past Spring

By Supreme Master Ching Hai in her late 20s
Originally in Aulacese (Vietnamese)

My sweet sister, do you ever dream about
Yellow apricot blossoms by the terrace in past springs?
I'm now in the West, so far away
Missing all very much in my heart!

My dear brother, do you ever dream about
Silk dresses, brocade shoes, and red firecrackers all over the city?
Young women, flowing tresses in the breeze,
Leisurely strolls on emerald grass, tender memories…

Last night I dreamt of my hometown
Seeing my brothers and sisters, so much to talk about!
Beside a bowl of savory spinach soup
And lullabies melodious as the rhythm of the swinging hammock…

Oh, how I miss the thatched house of old!
Mother, hair graying, gentle as the cool shade of coconut groves,
Father, dignified as in saintly kings' eras,
And Grandma's tasty meal that warmed the rainy winter!

And sisters and brothers and the fragrant rice field
And past adolescent love like a sad refrain!
All swept away by the bloody river of war
Dissolved in that evening of chaos long ago.

I stand amidst a snow-laden Western country,
Languishing for the grass by the breezy Perfume River!
The heavens pity and shed their tears,
Adding chill to the heart of someone far away from home!

Munich, Germany - Spring 1979
From the poetry collection: Traces of Previous Lives

YOU AND THE KINGDOM

Lyrics based on
Supreme Master Ching Hai's poem
Written in her youth

Rolf

from *The Real Love*
Music by Al Kasha

The Real Love

May - be it's the way that she smiles.

Ahh

Ahh

May - be it's the gen - tle tone from her lips or the

warmth and spar-kle of her eyes, I don't know what.

YOU AND THE KINGDOM

You and the Kingdom

By Supreme Master Ching Hai in her youth
Originally in English

It isn't the lovely kingdom
It is someone here that I love
Even with all the charm of la principauté
My heart wouldn't be here if you are not!

Ah! The illuminating mien
That brightens all corners of my thoughts
Also makes my mind restless
For no reason
No explanation!

Maybe it's the way you smile
Maybe it's the gentle tone from your lips
Or the warmth and blueness of your eyes...
I don't know what!
I just know that you are the most refined
And the most beautiful man
On the planet!

I see you everywhere
It's difficult to forget
I say hallo to your photos
I blow kisses
Through the windows.

Hi, hi! My Love
I am here, do you know?
I am here, so near
I am here because of you
Because I want to be with you so.

Some hidden magician
Has waved a magic wand
And separated our route
You are transported to the magnificent palace
While I am left somewhere else alone...

But he can never annul
The feeling that was once so strong!
We shall be patient:
One day will fade the mal potion
And the power of love will pervade
And that most beautiful face
That endearing aura
No longer stay afar...

The fairy tale
Ends happily ever after.

From the poetry collection: The Love of Centuries

MOON OF MINE

Lyrics based on
Supreme Master Ching Hai's poem

Thanh & Rolf

from *The Real Love*
Music by Bill Conti

The Real Love

MOON OF MINE

shine my path____ in the dark. You soothe my heart when____ I'm in

when I'm in pain.

pain, when I'm in pain.

MOON OF MINE

The Real Love

Moon of Mine

By Supreme Master Ching Hai
Originally in English

Oh moon of mine
How sweet your smile
Only for me
Oh how happy!

No one to see
No one to know
Our love for each other
Though you care for all!

No one can smile
So sweet and long
You are the one
You are the only one!

And when I'd sung
You stayed still and hung
Above the mountains
You listened and danced
Till my heart's content...
Endearing and lovely
You are the beauty
Of the galaxy.

You share the pain
And the joy, with me!
You are the loyal
Friend of eternity.

You shine my path
In the dark mountain
You soothe my heart
When I'm in pain.

Can any one
See any thing
More beautiful than you!

I wait for you
In time of waning
In cloudy nights
In stormy skies.

You have to be
In my existence.
What's life without
My moon?!

I will not exchange
The world's treasure
For just half of you
Shining beauty
Stay forever and ever
In the vast sky...

The world loves you
And I love you
Thank you for being
The best of friends!

I love you, Moon.
I love you, Moon!
I love you forever
My Moon.

From the poetry collection:
The Love of Centuries

I BELIEVE ONLY IN LOVE

Lyrics based on
Supreme Master Ching Hai's poem
Written in her youth

Wedding Singer

from *The Real Love*
Music by Al Kasha

hearts will not shi-ver de-spite the rag-ing storm._____ I be-lieve on - ly in

love.

love_____ Love_____ on-ly in love.

love_____ Love_____ on-ly in love.

When in love___ no one minds ex-ter-nal scenes. Ev' - ry-where is Hea - ven. Ev'-

Ev' - ry-where is Hea-

Ev' - ry-where is Hea-

When We're in Love

By Supreme Master Ching Hai in her youth
Originally in Aulacese (Vietnamese)

Darling, can you see we are like a pair of swallows,
Soaring in the endless sky?
Can you see we are as butterflies
In a spring garden fragrant with life's blooms?
Can you see we are like the river,
Flowing broadly toward the open sea?

Because we are in love, the Earth is so ravishing,
Because we are in love, the world becomes joyful!

I believe only in love,
Everything else on Earth lacks meaning.
Even if this world is leveled to the ground,
Even if the seas dry up and mountains wear down,
Love will live forever in the infinite universe.

Just to love each other,
Loving each other is enough.

Then our souls will flourish, assured.
Walking amid turmoil and misery as if in Heaven,
Our hearts will not shiver despite the raging storm.

When in love,
No one minds external scenes;
Everywhere is Heaven.
The couple is
Eve and Adam!

From the poetry collection: Pebbles and Gold

 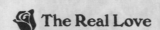

SINCE WE KNEW EACH OTHER

Lyrics based on
Supreme Master Ching Hai's
poem written in 1979
Calmbach, Germany

Company

from *The Real Love*
Music by Don Pippin

In your si-lent man-ner I found my-self. In your qui-et style is re-born my peace.

Ma-ny dark nights, soft and tran-quil Your voice ten-der calms my

Since We Knew Each Other

By Supreme Master Ching Hai in her late 20s
Originally in English

In your silent manner I found myself,
In your quiet style is reborn my peace:
Many dark nights, soft and tranquil,
Your voice tender calms my madness!

O lover of grand amour!
From reincarnation and a thousand promises!
Do you still remember,
Our love lives before?...

...There were boring love affairs, weary adventures,
While I was hurriedly sailing to true happiness.
So many times in the chaotic world
I was lost and perplexed.

But gone now are the stormy days:
Your love like spring water cools my burning heart!
It's over, the long voyage,
Here I've arrived to stay.

Calmbach, Germany - 1979
From the poetry collection: The Lost Memories

WEEKEND THOUGHTS

Thanh

Lyrics based on
Supreme Master Ching Hai's
poem written in 1979
Allach, Germany

from *The Real Love*
Music by Don Pippin

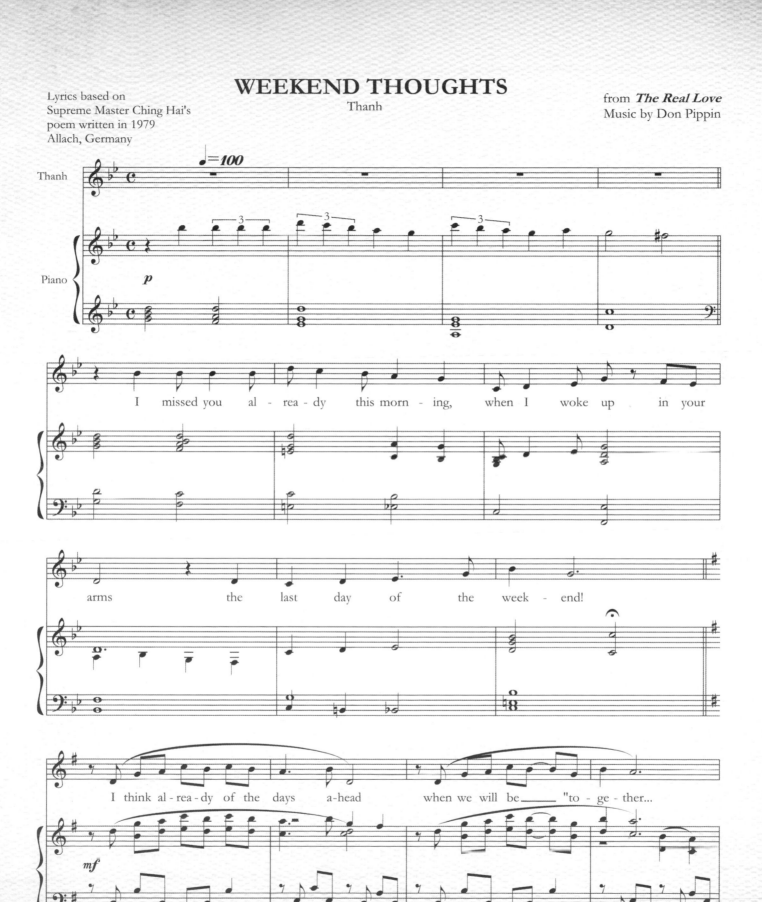

Weekend Thoughts

By Supreme Master Ching Hai in her late 20s
Originally in English

I missed you already this morning
When I woke up in your arms,
The last day of the weekend!

I think already
Of the days ahead
When we will be "together...
But in two places" again!

... And when I am far away from you
Doubts and loneliness fly in through the window!
I just can't think of anything else
But throw everything away and run to you.
But do you ever
Ever want me to?...

Allach, Germany - August 1979
From the poetry collection: The Lost Memories

SELF CONFESSION

Lyrics based on
Supreme Master Ching Hai's
poem written in 1980, Italy

Elsa

from *The Real Love*
Music by David Shire

ma - ny strug-gles I a-wake sud-den-ly___ Ask-ing my-self, "Is that all there is?"

What does it mat-ter, a few ex-tra tens of years, To chase for fame and gain with ef-forts so dear!

What shall I do in the days a-head, When hair los-es lus-ter and youth-ful ros-i-ness fades? When

breath-ing ceas-es, is it death or re - birth?

Self Confession

By Supreme Master Ching Hai in her early 30s
Originally in Aulacese (Vietnamese)

I've lived through days of deception,
Professing love not felt genuinely!
Sweet utterances from rosy lips,
Passionate words from an ice cold heart…

So many times, I've lost and gained,
Waning strength in exchange for an ephemeral existence!
This body, a grave for thousands of beings:
Many lives perished to sustain my existence!

I've indulged in many illusions,
Day and night, keeping up with the Joneses.
This ephemeral body, skin burning with passion,
How I writhed, plunging into the fire of lust!!

I've passed many shores, clear and muddy,
Washing my face, then painting it again,
Desiring fame, fine houses and wealth,
To enjoy this life, I've abandoned noble ideals…

After many struggles, I awake suddenly
Asking myself, "Is that all there is?"
What does it matter, a few extra tens of years,
To chase for fame and gain with efforts so dear!

What shall I do in the days ahead,
When hair loses luster and youthful rosiness fades?
When breathing ceases, is it death or rebirth?
Christ and Buddha taught about Heaven and purgatory!

I ask myself in this self confession today:
Is this life, or is death close by?

Italy · 1980
From the poetry collection: The Old Time

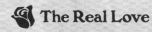 **The Real Love**

SEARCH HIGH AND LOW

Lyrics based on
Supreme Master Ching Hai's
poems written in her youth

Greta

from *The Real Love*
Music by Don Pippin

SEARCH HIGH AND LOW

Ri - ding co - los - sal waves, fly - ing through gray - ing for - ests.

Charg - ing in - to the fe - roc - ious wind, cross - ing the stor - my sky!

Search high and low for a lit - tle love.

Search high and low for a lit - tle love.

Search High and Low

Excerpts from poems written
by Supreme Master Ching Hai in her youth

Search high and low
For a little love,
For a little love!
To bestow on all beings
In all corners of existence!

Riding colossal waves
Flying through graying forests
Charging into the ferocious wind
Crossing the stormy sky!

Search high and low
For a little love,
For a little love!

You have to breathe
The air of Heaven
You have to go
Where the wind blows

Fly with the birds
Rise with the sun

Look into the heart of a flower
And find God there.

Search high and low
For a little love,
For a little love!

Search high and low
For a little love,
For a little love!
To bestow on all beings
on all beings!

"There Were Disappointing Times"
Originally in Aulacese (Vietnamese)
From the poetry collection: Wu Tzu Poems

"Lone Journey"
Originally in Aulacese (Vietnamese)
From the poetry collection: Wu Tzu Poems

"Screaming Out Loud"
From the poetry collection: The Old Time

"Thanksgiving"
Originally in Aulacese (Vietnamese)
From the poetry collection: The Dream of a Butterfly

FOR THE ONE WHO STAYED BEHIND

Thanh & Rolf

Lyrics based on Supreme Master Ching Hai's
poems written in the early 1980s
Munich, Germany

from *The Real Love*
Music by David Shire

The Real Love

brass, I would sof-ten and melt as I feel the pain I left you._____ But be-

I would sof-ten and melt as I feel the pain I left you._____

lov-ed one,__ I can no long-er stay in dark-ness, sur-ren-der-ing to ig-nor-ance and mis-er-y.

I know you've been suf-fer-ing in gold-en bond, long-ing to be free._____ I

The Real Love

"*The play was beautiful. It was so heartfelt and emotional. The last song of the first part ('For the One Who Stayed Behind') just touched me.*"

BEVERLY POMERANTZ
Casting director

For the One Who Stayed Behind

By Supreme Master Ching Hai in her early 30s
Originally in Aulacese (Vietnamese)

When you come home,
There will be only grass and flowers
Greeting your footsteps!
The garden sheds her evening dew,
The house bows weighed in loneliness,
Murmuring farewell!

Even if my heart were made of stone
And my feelings of brass,
They would be softened and melt
Thinking of the pain I've left you!

But beloved one!
I can no longer stay in darkness,
Surrendering to ignorance and misery.
Don't you know I've been suffering in golden bond
Longing to be free?

Praised be the Buddha whose light guides my way,
And protects you in your lonely days.

Why were we born in this world of woe
For you to pine, for me to taste sorrow!?
Since which era have we pledged our faithful vows,
Thus bind ourselves in matrimony now?

Please lift your heart out of the blue web
So my mind will also be lightened when we are apart.
Praised be the Buddha whose light guides my way,
And protects the one who stays behind!

One day, I'll be enlightened and bring illumination to the world,
We will be together for eternity...

Munich, Germany - early 1980s
From the poetry collection: The Dream of a Butterfly

I Love You

By Supreme Master Ching Hai in her early 30s
Originally in Aulacese (Vietnamese)

I love you as I love myself
Like my love for the five continents, great Earth, mountains and rivers
Tomorrow's farewell, who will shed tears?
I bow to you in awe of your deep love!
Who knows when we'll ever meet again–
Sorrow for you with hair still lush
yet the color of amour has turned gray.
I'm leaving, aspired to reach Heaven high
Vowing to level out all upheavals in life!

Munich, Germany - early 1980s
From the poetry collection: Wu Tzu Poems

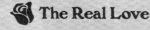 The Real Love

WELCOME TO INDIA

Company

Lyrics by Frank Evans

from *The Real Love*
Music by Doug Katsaros

The Real Love

WELCOME TO INDIA

WELCOME TO INDIA

THE GOD SEEKER

Thanh & Company

Lyrics based on Supreme Master Ching Hai's
poem written in the early 1980s
McLeod Ganj, India

from *The Real Love*
Music by Bill Conti

The Real Love

The God Seeker

By Supreme Master Ching Hai in her early 30s
Originally in Aulacese (Vietnamese)

I've been searching for the Buddha everywhere
Casting aside riches and comfort,
Leaving behind my possessions and beloved!
Abandoning life like a roadside inn,
Are but a comedy show – success and fame!

I've been searching for the Buddha's return
But mountains are high and the seas vast,
Where can Thou be?
The world is in darkness and filled with misery
Innumerable beings thirst for Thee.

Namo Maitreya Muni
Have compassion for all sentient beings in darkness:
Divine halo enlightens the ignorant
Descending on Earth to save those languishing!

McLeod Ganj, India - early 1980s
From the poetry collection: Wu Tzu Poems

P.S. TILL TOMORROW

Lyrics based on
Supreme Master Ching Hai's
poem written in the early 1980s

Thanh

from *The Real Love*
Music by David Shire

🌹 **The Real Love**

think... I'll buy___ a pair of hu-man ears for You to-mor - row._____ In

case You've lost the hu-man heart, please take mine. So You may sym-pa-thize with all my

fel - low be - ings on the same boat___ who long for Nir - va___ na,___

But all they know is sor - row.

P.S. Till Tomorrow

By Supreme Master Ching Hai in her early 30s
Originally in English

Your door is forever forbidden
Every time I approach
It shuts aloof and cold!
The curtains are drawn.
There is a dim light inside but never once Your face.
I know You are in the Palace.
Just can't open the door.
I think one day I'll bring along a big hammer!

Master! Do You have ears at all?
You must!
In order to hear my desperate call.
I think...
I'll buy a pair of human ears for You
Tomorrow.

In the case that You've lost Your human heart,
Please take mine.
So that You may sympathize
With all my fellow beings who are on the same boat,
Who long for Nirvana,
But all they know is samsara.

Here are my human eyes offered to You with gladness,
Please wear them all twenty-four hours.
So You might once see
How I've become so weary

While walking the lonely path,
Forever searching for a glimpse
Of Your beauty

I'm tired!
Heartbroken.
Have no more patience.
After all, I'm only a frail mortal, You know it!
I quit.

P.S. Till tomorrow.

Early 1980s
Excerpt from the poetry collection: Silent Tears

DO YOU MISS ME, DARLING

Rolf

Lyrics based on
Supreme Master Ching Hai's
poem written in her youth

from *The Real Love*
Music by Bill Conti

DO YOU MISS ME, DARLING

Sea - gulls _____ are fly - ing low, boats toss and turn.

The bay this eve - ning seems so dis - tant. Do you miss me,

dar - ling? Do you miss me, dar - ling? _____ As nights

pass and days go by I miss on - ly you, all the time! Do you miss me,

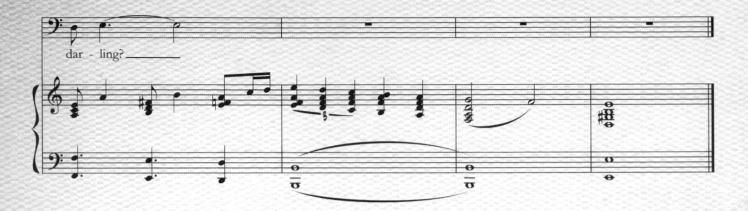

dar - ling? _____

The Real Love

Do You Miss...

By Supreme Master Ching Hai in her youth
Originally in Aulacese (Vietnamese)

When you're there
And I am here,
Do you miss me, my precious,
The one with beautiful eyes?

The river continues flowing,
The rose bush is sad and lonely.
Clutching the single pillow,
I dream of our glorious time together.

It's no fun to live an empty life,
To long for someone far away!
Do you miss me, my dearest,
The one with luscious lips?

Seagulls are flying low, aimlessly
And boats sadly toss and turn here and there!
The bay this evening seems so distant.
Your every breath I'm missing!

As nights pass and days float by,
I can't cease thinking of you!...

From the poetry collection: Pebbles and Gold

 **The Real Love**

ON THE RIVERBANK

Thanh

Lyrics and Music by
Supreme Master Ching Hai
Composed in the early 1980s
Ganges River, India

from *The Real Love*

ON THE RIVERBANK

when you spoke of the suff'-ring in this world. You make my life

flow-ing_____ like the ri - ver wa - ter. Then to -

mor - row we'll reach the sea - shore..._____ I_____

love_____ to sit on the ri-ver-bank re-mem-ber-ing the

tears in your eyes when you spoke of_____ the suf-fer-ing in this world.

On the Riverbank

By Supreme Master Ching Hai in her early 30s
Originally in English

I would love to sit on the riverbank
Listening to the sound of water
And the birds.

I would love to sit on the riverbank
Looking at the flowing water
And hear the songs within...

You make my life flowing
Like the river water.
Then tomorrow
We'll reach the seashore...

I would love to sit on the riverbank
Remembering the tears in your eyes
When you spoke of
The suffering in this world.

Ganges River, India - early 1980s
From the poetry collection: The Dream of a Butterfly

IF IT WASN'T FOR SPROUTS IN LIFE

Lyrics based on
Supreme Master Ching Hai's
poem written in Autumn 1979
Munich, Germany

Klaus

from *The Real Love*
Music by Don Pippin

The Real Love

If it wasn't for sprouts in li-fe   Oh where to would I have run?   May-be to a mo-nas-te-ry___   But

there I must be   so lone-ly,___   like a monk   with-out a nun.

(Tap Dance)

If There Wasn't You in Life

By Supreme Master Ching Hai in her late 20s
Originally in English

If there wasn't you in life
I would have gone to the moon,
Sitting there miserable
Like a dog without bones!

If there wasn't you in life
I would have been so lonesome;
Think of the sunflower
Without the shining sun!

If there wasn't you in life
Where to would I have gone?
Maybe to a monastery
But there I must be so lonely
Like a nun without a monk!

Munich, Germany - Autumn 1979
From the poetry collection: The Lost Memories

OUR TIME

Lyrics based on
Supreme Master Ching Hai's
poem written in her 20s

Thanh & Rolf

from *The Real Love*
Music by Al Kasha

The Real Love

It's an amazing story for someone to fall in love like Supreme Master Ching Hai did and then to have to leave that to follow a greater path. What a lesson. There were a number of times when I teared in the show."

STORMY SACKS
Composer

The Real Love

Our Time

By Supreme Master Ching Hai in her 20s
Originally in English

The time we spend together
I will always treasure
Do not forget our memory
For love is the one and only.

Who says the world is ephemeral?
If we are together it's eternal.
Dream and life merge in unison
When our souls are one.

The peace within is the peace without
Heaven will be here and now!
For those who have found true love
Flowers of Eden bloom in their souls.

We live in God, we live in men,
We live in happiness that never ends.
We walk in beauty, we walk in bliss
We laugh, we sing to our heart's content.

Forget me not, forget us not
For us is all that we got.
What else is there for one to hold
To fill the emptiness in our souls?

The love we share is the love we save,
Love from Heaven descends to Earth.
The love in you, the love in me
Is the love of God that ever be!

From the poetry collection: The Dream of a Butterfly

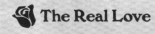 **The Real Love**

GANGA MA

Lyrics by Frank Evans

Company

from *The Real Love*

Music by Doug Katsaros

The Real Love

Splash the wa - ter on___ your face. Dip your hands, plunge your feet,

Splash the wa - ter on___ your face. Dip your hands, plunge your feet,

plunge your face and hands and feet. Let all of your sins be cleansed.

plunge your face and hands and feet. Let all of your sins be cleansed.

GANGA MA

THE PEACE SEEKER

Company

Lyrics based on
Supreme Master Ching Hai's
poem written in the early 1980s

from *The Real Love*
Music by Bill Conti

The Peace Seeker

By Supreme Master Ching Hai in her early 30s
Originally in English

Once upon a time,
A true peace lover wandered around the many worlds
     in search of eternal happiness.
She walked over the face of the earth,
The suns, the moons and the clouds.
At last she found:
That it was all the while
Hidden in her very heart.
Then she sat down
And was about to enjoy the newfound Bliss.
But suddenly she looked down:
And saw countless beings were still groveling in darkness,
For they were searching for happiness without,
Just like her before, erring over millions of ages.
Her tears were then rolling down...
     One drop,
     two drops...
     and many more...
Each drop became a shining Jewel
     and soon the firmament was studded with glittering tears
     which are the stars today;
They are too shy in the day
     and too restless in the night
     to go to sleep.
For all peace seekers,
The stars are there to light the Way
And to remind them of the Compassion of a holy Sage.

Early 1980s
Excerpt from the poetry collection: Silent Tears

 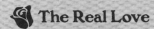

I cried at the end, and I loved it. And the production value is incredible. The last number ('The Peace Seeker') was beautiful, and I was in tears. I felt a catharsis with the character, and that was a wonderful moment.

I've had the honor and privilege of meeting the Supreme Master. And she is real. There are a lot of people in the world who speak like she does, but they don't mean it. She means it. She is so full of love and generosity and kindness and understanding."

CARY BROWN (Vegan)
Three-time Emmy Award-winning filmmaker
41st California State Assembly District Delegate, USA

I would just like to say thank you, Supreme Master, very, very much for all you have done for humanity and are still doing for humanity. And thank you very much for this beautiful, beautiful musical that came from your poetry and your love of humanity. We thank you. All of us thank you."

SHIRLEY JONES
Academy Award-winning actress/singer

"This was one of the most beautiful, inspiring moments."

CAROL CONNORS
Two-time Academy Award-nominated songwriter/singer

"I have learned through The Real Love musical that Supreme Master Ching Hai's real compassion and love toward a suffering humanity led her to leave her happy marriage and a secure life in search of spiritual enlightenment.

The Earth has still been preserved up till now thanks to the genuine love of Supreme Master Ching Hai and all on the planet. We need more love in the future in order to preserve the Earth in health.

I agree with Supreme Master Ching Hai's message that putting veganism into practice is the real love in this era."

DR. LEE JAE-YONG
10th Minister of Environment, Republic of Korea

"The Real Love sings and enchants our hearts and enlightens our spirits...."

EVELYNE CHRIST-DASSAS
Actress, France

"*Supreme Master Ching Hai is a remarkable lady.* I mean, she is very holy but not in any formal religious way. I was very impressed by that.

I liked a lot of her poetry as singing, reminded me of Bob Dylan. And I liked that. It was real, it was committed, it wasn't phony. And I felt the instincts of the actors, and of her personal journey, were true."

MICHAEL LERNER
Academy Award-nominated actor

"It's so incredible. And it was a really heartwarming, lovely, sweet story that I can't imagine anyone not loving it. It was such a gift that you have that feeling after a night like this that you want to do something good... thinking more than just about yourself; to think about the whole picture of humanity."

TERESA GANZEL
Voice actress (WALL-E, Monsters, Inc.)

"The real love for me is love for your fellow man and your fellow creatures, to love all the many creatures in the animal kingdom. I am very much behind the vegetarian activism and everything of the Supreme Master."

ED BEGLEY, JR. (Vegan)
Six-time Emmy Award-nominated actor

*"**The play was wonderful.** It actually is one of the better Broadway-type plays I've seen in quite a while, so I was very pleased with it.*

What ran through my mind were the many different definitions of The Real Love. First thing to me is that God is the provider of the real love and it's up to us to really carry that out. And that was something like Supreme Master's message as well."

DON WUEBBLES, PH.D
Professor of Atmospheric Sciences
Nobel Peace Prize laureate

"The musical The Real Love has been produced with much love to detail, with lightness and dedication. It's amazing, the participation of such outstanding artists.

The music and the stage setting are a reflection of the sensitivity and also of the love for life. Her whole life story is depicted in a wonderfully theatrical way. It touches everybody who sees it.

It is a great challenge to depict the eventful life of such a great personality like the Supreme Master Ching Hai in a musical, but here it has been a success.

I hope that through this musical, the message of love, of mutual respect and respect for nature and all beings reaches many people of the world. Supreme Master Ching Hai is an example for all of us."

HER ROYAL HIGHNESS
PRINCESS MAJA VON HOHENZOLLERN
of Germany

*"**It was such a genuine and** captivating story and performed with such love – it was a true gift to see! I left genuinely inspired and so grateful – not simply to have 'seen' a musical, but to have experienced a work of art made so purely from love."*

LEAH GRIMSSON (Vegan)
American actress

The Red Love

This is once-in-a-lifetime that we can see all these great people together in one cast, in one musical. I can never thank all of you enough for your incredible, loving dedication and support to art and love. This is the real love – your love.

Love is the most precious thing in this physical realm. So we must protect love, be it the love between a couple, between parents and children, between friends, love between humans or love between animals, love between humans and animals; be it even the love between plants and trees. Real love is what we need to protect our world, especially now.

If we have love, all good will come our way. Love the animals – we'll be veg. Love the Earth – we'll go green. Love the world – save the planet.

Be vegan, make peace. That's all we have to do, and love."

—**Supreme Master Ching Hai**
August 27, 2011
Supreme Master Television's 5th Anniversary: The Real Love

269

Interviews about THE REAL LOVE

Announcements in the MEDIA

"Real Love" Extravaga

By Ted AYALA

One of the biggest events of the year is about to arrive. An all-day
festival of music and art is coming to the Pasadena Civic Auditorium or
Saturday, Aug. 27. The world premiere of a new musical, "The Real Lo
created by an all-star team of composers and lyricists and starring som
Broadway's most brilliant talent. Capping off the event will be American
beloved s

originating in E
Re
and

Vietna
which
a pari
living
vega
in Alh
Hai ha
recog

Inspire
the lov
the he
surren
of the
film ar
recipie

Broadway   Tours
Off-Bway   London
Help, Pick Me a Show

philSTAR.com
The Filipino Global Community

THE PHILIPPINE STAR | PILIPINO STAR NGAYON | THE FREE
HOME | HEADLINES | OPINION | NATION | METRO | BUSINESS | SPORTS

BREAKING NEWS
ENTERTAINMENT

Joanna Ampil with Adam Pasca
musical concert The Real Love

By Girlie Rodis (The Philippine Star) Updated September 27, 2011 12:0

MANILA, Philippines - Joanna

Home | Playbill Club | News | Listings | Features | Store | Cast

Diva Talk | Brief En

News: U.S./Canada

Brows
Sectio

Real Love, With Betty Buckley, Shirley Jones, Cac
Huffman, Adam Pascal, Will Be Broadcast Sept. 2

By *Andrew Gans*
16 Sep 2011

The world premiere of *The Real Love:
New Musical*, which was presented Au
27 at the Pasadena Civic Auditorium,
will be rebroadcast on Supreme Mast
Television in nine parts, beginning Se
26, with multi-language subtitles.

Live online streaming can be viewed
www.SupremeMasterTV.com.

Directed by LA Drama Critics Circle
Award winner Chris Shelton, the

UNITED STATES | THE WORLD | GUIDES | SPECIAL OFFERS

THE REAL LOVE Debuts at Pasadena Civic,
Broadcasts Live

f Like 4 | Tweet 6 | +1 0 | 🔖 Feedback 🖨 Print ✉ E-mail

Enter Your Email | Subscribe to Alerts for this Author

Friday, September 9, 2011; 08:09 PM - by BWW News De

Over 3,000 people gave a rousing standing ovation for the wo
premiere of "The Real Love," a new musical which brought
together some of the biggest names of Hollywood and Broadw
onstage at the Pasadena Civic. In what may be the first time i
musical theater history, the opening of "The Real Love" was a
experienced by worldwide television viewers watching the live
broa
was
pro

◀ Buck Henry, John Kelly
to Appear in John...
THEATER NEWS

Hollywood Today:
rch, type and hit enter
w Direct RSS Feed:
Hollywood Today
RSS Feed to:
AOL | My Google
MSN | My Yahoo
Join Mailing List:
Subscribe

NT STORIES
Bowl Annual Playboy
stival Playboy Lineup
ced for 2012
rdo Live" Exhibits
Collection of Da Vinci

hanting Evening with
Perlman
GRILL RESTAURANT
E HOTEL
CONTINENTAL
a Liar Live on
adio Meet the Music
th
nage Award Noms for
ast Among You
ck Cafe' Debuts Style

Bowl XLVI – vs – A No
or the manufacturers
CARTER, HALL OF
CATCHER, DIES OF
CANCER AT 57
ason Bateman and
anda Anka Welcome
irl
– Too Short

Supreme Master TV celebrates
its 5th anniversary with
'The Real Love'

f Like | Digg | Submit | Tweet 7

HOLLYWOOD,CA (Hollywood Today) 8/16/11/—Tony Award
nominees & winners Daisy Eagan, Cady Huffman, Adam Pascal, Robert
Torti and Betty Buckley will star in the new Broadway style musical.

Music by Oscar winners Al Kasha, Bill Conti, Grammy winner David
Shire, Emmy winner Don Pippin and Emmy nominee Doug Katsaros.
The celebration will also include a concert by legendary performer Don
McLean. Pre art exhibit by world renowned Supreme Master Ching Hai.

Pasadena,CA- The Supreme Master Television network celebrates its
5th anniversary with a star studded Broadway style original musical in
a one time performance and a concert by Don McLean and art
exhibition. Saturday August 27, starting at 12 pm at the Pasadena Civic
Auditorium, 300 East Green Street, Pasadena, CA.

Supreme Master TV's headquarters are located in southern California.
Supreme Master Ching Hai is the inspiration for this incredible network
airing constructive news and programs that foster peace and promote
healthy green living.

This amazing musical, concert and art exhibit is a must-see for
everyone. In addition to the stars performing, many stars will be
attending this event. Media will be updated on a weekly basis.

All media is welcomed to attend. Live shots are welcome. Coverage
will include: red carpet arrivals, arrivals of the stars to the post VIP
party inside the Pasadena Civic, and limited performance footage. Stars
that have confirmed to attend this event are below and will be updated
weekly.

Daisy Eagan, Cady Huffman
Pascal, et al. set for *The Rea*

By Dan Bacalzo • Aug 2, 2011 • Los Angeles

Joanna Ampil, Daisy Eagan, Cady Huffman, Adam Pascal and
Robert Torti will star in a presentation of *The Real Love: A
New Musical* at the Pasadena Civic Auditorium on Saturday,
August 27 at 2pm. Chris Shelton will direct.

In the musical, the poetry of Supreme Master Ching Hai is set
to music by Bill Conti, Al Kasha, Doug Katsaros, Don Pippin,
and David Shire. The show is inspired by a true story about a
woman who is deeply in love with her equally tender husband,
a doctor. But as their happy marriage blossoms, a calling
propels her to make a heartrending decision - remain with her
beloved or sacrifice everything in search of happiness for all
humanity.

Special guest stars will include Betty Buckley, Laurie Cadevida,
Filippa Giordano, Marty Ingels, Shirley Jones, Trent Kowalik,
Kiril Kulish, Faith Rivera, Tom Schmid, and Lynne Winterstelle

The two-part show will also include a set by Don McLean and h
time classic hits, such as "And I Love You So", "American Pie",

For tickets and more information, click here.

Discover 'The Real Love' In
Pasadena Saturday

STUDIO CITY (CBS) — "The Real Love," a Broadway style musical,
is coming to Los Angeles for a one night only performance!

Al Kasha, who helped write the musical, visited the KCAL 9 studios
Tuesday.

The musical is a part of the Supreme Master Television Network's 5th

Sunday

Los Angeles Times

latimes.com

SUNDAY, JULY 17, 2011

$1.50 DESIGNATED AREAS HIGHER   308 PAGES   © 2011 WST

SUPREME MASTER TV'S 2-PART ANNIVERSARY SHOW

"The Real Love" New Musical Comes to The Pasadena Civic

"The Real Love: A New Musical" is a new Broadway-style musical inspired by a true love story, featuring a Tony Award-winning cast (40 members total!).

You can see its one-time special showing at the prestigious Pasadena Civic Auditorium on August 27, as part of Supreme Master Television's 5th anniversary celebration – a 2-part entertainment which will also include a live concert by Don McLean ("American Pie").

Directed by Chris Shelton, winner of the LA Drama Critics Circle Award, "The Real Love" stars Tony winner **Daisy Eagan** (lead role in "The Secret Garden"), Tony winner **Cady Huffman** (Mel Brooks' "The Producers"), and Tony nominee **Adam Pascal** ("Rent"), and Tony nominee **Robert Torti** ("Starlight Express").

Special guest stars will be Tony winner **Betty Buckley** (original cast of "Cats"), Italian classical/pop star **Filippa Giordano**, Oscar winner **Shirley Jones** ("Oklahoma!," "The Partridge Family"), Tony winners **Trent Kowalik** and **Kiril Kulish** ("Billy Elliot"), Emmy winning singer **Faith Rivera**, actor and singer **Tom Schmid**, soprano **Lynne Wintersteller**, and veteran actor **Dick Van Patten**.

The music, played by a 20-piece orchestra, is by five award-winning composers. Among them, Oscar & 5-time Emmy winner **Bill Conti** (19-time Music Director of the Academy Awards), said: "Something is more intuitively better in music to inspire you into going to peace... When music really works, it works at that level." America's sought-after theater and film composers – namely, **Bill Conti** ("Rocky"), 2-time Oscar winner **Al Kasha** ("The Poseidon Adventure"), Emmy nominee **Doug Katsaros** ("Footloose"), Tony & Emmy winner **Don Pippin** ("Oliver!"), and Oscar & 2-time Grammy winner **David Shire** ("Baby"), contributed the songs which set to music the brilliant, moving poetry of **Supreme Master Ching Hai**, world-renowned humanitarian, spiritual leader, poet, and artist.

"I take a kind of playwright's approach to writing songs," says David Shire. "It's a growing emotion, and that is as much the lyricist's responsibility as the composer's. It's probably because of the largeness of the Supreme Master's soul that she has the kind of largeness of artistic temperament."

The 2-part show will also present the legendary Don McLean in concert, performing his all-time favorite songs such as "And I Love You So," "Vincent (Starry Starry Night)," and his 1971 No. 1 hit "American Pie."

You'll also enjoy a complimentary dinner banquet catered by LA's premier vegan restaurants: Loving Hut and One Veg World. Arrive early for a celebrity red carpet, refreshments, and an art exhibition of Supreme Master Ching Hai's uplifting creations. The event will be broadcast later on Supreme Master Television. Order tickets soon for this one-time only special engagement!

What:
Don McLean in Concert &
The Real Love: A New Musical

Where:
Pasadena Civic Auditorium

When:
2 PM Saturday, August 27

Tickets:
$35–55
1.800.745.3000
Ticketmaster.com

Information:
1.626.623.2225
www.TheRealLoveMusic.com

"new Broadway-style musical inspired by a true love story"

Daisy Eagan
Tony winner

Cady Huffman
Tony winner

Adam Pascal
Tony nominee

Robert Torti
Tony nominee

Don McLean
Legendary singer-songwriter

Betty Buckley
Tony winner

Shirley Jones
Oscar winner

SUPREME MASTER TELEVISION'S
5TH ANNIVERSARY / 2-PART ENTERTAINMENT

ASADENA STAR-NEWS

Best of Pasadena, Whittier and the San Gabriel Valley

TODAY 96/67 • TOMORROW 96/72 • Full weather Page A16

features@sgvn.com

LOVE MUSICAL
Tony winner Eagan takes stage.
STORY Page 3

EEKEND

an brings a love
y to the stage

OVE: A NEW

...day
...les 14 and older
...ivic Auditorium,
...en St., Pasadena
...225

...eallovemusic.com
...mentary banquet
...y Loving Hut and
...d Vegan Cuisine is
...ter the performance.

...elle J. Mills
...iter

...e 11, Daisy Eagan
... as she accepted the
...ward for "Best Perfor-
...by a Featured Actress
...usical" for her role in
...ecret Garden." The Los
...es resident kept busy on
... like "The Wild Party"
..."Misar bles" and TV

Eagan plays Greta, the woman's friend, who advises her to visit India in hopes of refining her faith.

"I would say that the overall message is about the power of love, not just between people, but between people and whatever their higher power is and how restorative and powerful that love and faith can be," Eagan said. "It's about the power of love to change lives."

Eagan identifies with Greta, as the character loves life and is always looking to learn more. Greta's passion was art, but she pursued medicine until her creativity called her back, much like Eagan's tug-of-war between careers.

Eagan left acting with the goal of becoming a therapist and now has degrees in psychology and creative writing.
Since her return to acting.

NGUOI V
CƠ QUAN TRANH ĐẤU THỜI SỰ VĂN NG
SUNDAY, SEPTEMBER 25, 2011 CHỦ NHẬT 25 tháng 9-2011 - NĂM THỨ 33 - SỐ 9423 -

Scan camera của điện thoại vào "QR Code" này
để vào thẳng www.nguoi-viet.com

經濟
中華民國100年9月25日 ★ 星期日 農曆辛卯年8月28日
【台北訊】為慶祝
無上師慶生 真愛音樂繼...

PASADENA'S ROSE magazine

NOV-DEC 2011

Real love
for peace

Supreme Master Television — an international nonprofit channel airing news and programs that foster peace and promote healthy, green living — celebrated its fifth anniversary on Aug. 27 with a two-part show, "The Real Love Musical" and "Don McLean in Concert," at the Pasadena Civic Auditorium.

CRESC...

W...
THE FOOTH...

SEPTEMBER 15, 2011

Big Names Cele...
"The Real Lo...

Gourmet plant-based fare served to thousands as part of Supreme Master TV's anniversary.

story, starr...
actress Joa...
Eagan, Ca...
Pascal and...
songs and...
from tap...
the audie...

More than...

AZAZEL JACOBS' MISFIT TEEN FLICK | FOSTER THE PEOPLE'S PUMPED-UP POP | THE CRA BRINGS BLIGHT TO MID-CITY

WEEKLY

PASADENA
Weekly

08.25.11 pasadenaweekly.com GREATER PASADENA'S FREE NEWS AND ENTERT... EKLY

BEST PASADEN... BALLOT INSIDE

Starry,
starry night

DON MCLEAN HEADLINES CELEBRITY-FILLED SHOW BRINGING 'THE REAL LOVE' TO SUPREME MASTER T...
BY CARL KOZLOWSKI

PRIME PICK

IT'S NOT OFTEN THAT OLD HOLLYWOOD STARS TEAM UP FOR A NEW AGE entertainment event. But that unlikely combination will indeed come together Saturday for a one-time-only spectacle at the Pasadena Civic Auditorium, as the Internet-streamed Supreme Master TV channel presents the star-studded musical "The Real Love," preceded by a concert from perennial favorite singer-songwriter Don McLean.

The event, which includes a vegan buffet dinner after the performances, celebrates the fifth anniversary of the Web-based programming outlet suprememastertv.com, which also airs across North America via the Galaxy 19 satellite. The nonprofit enterprise focuses on "constructive news and programs that foster peace and healthy green living," says Dawn Salomon, the media rep for Supreme Master TV.

"Since starting in 2006, it's around the world with 14 satellite platforms on 90 cab... and IPTV networks. We also have over 40 subtitles for languages," says Salomon. The channel is inspired by Supreme Master Ching Hai...

1. **Tom Schmid**, actor/singer
2. **Leah Grimsson & Sasha Stuber**, actresses (vegan)
3. **Dee Wallace**, actress (*E.T.: The Extra-Terrestial*)
4. **Steve Lee Jones**, Golden Globe & Emmy Award-nominated film producer
5. **Lynne Wintersteller**, soprano
6. **Doris Roberts**, five-time Emmy Award-winning actress
7. **Don McLean**, American icon singer/songwriter
8. **Shirley Jones**, Academy Award-winning actress
9. **Michael Lerner**, Academy Award-nominated actor
10. **Faith Rivera**, Emmy Award-winning singer/songwriter
11. **Teresa Ganzel**, voice actress (*WALL-E, Monsters, Inc.*)
12. **Carol Connors**, two-time Academy Award-nominated songwriter/singer
13. **Ed Begley, Jr.**, six-time Emmy Award-nominated actor (vegan)
14. **Daisy Eagan**, Tony Award-winning actress
15. **Florence LaRue**, Grammy Award-winning singer
16. **Brittany Alexis Palmer**, actress (*All My Children*)
17. **Abigail Mason**, award-winning actress

18. **Kim Poirier**, actress
19. **David "Shark" Fralick**, actor (*The Young and the Restless*)
20. **Grant Aleksander**, four-time Emmy Award-nominated actor (*All My Children*) (vegetarian)
21. **Frank Stallone**, Golden Globe & Grammy Award-nominated songwriter & actor
22. **Hayley Marie Norman**, film actress & model (*Deal or No Deal*) (vegan)
23. **Cady Huffman**, Tony Award-winning actress
24. **Dominic Pace**, award-winning actor
25. **Adam Pascal**, Tony Award-nominated actor

26. **Erin Murphy**, TV actress (*Bewitched*)
27. **Joanna Ampil**, award-winning actress/singer
28. **Howard Fishman**, Honorable Mayor of Hermosa Beach, California, USA
29. **Julianna Rose**, Emmy Award-nominated actress (*LazyTown*)
30. **Robert Torti**, Tony Award-winning actor
31. **Don Wuebbles**, PhD, Professor of Atmospheric Sciences, Nobel Peace Prize laureate
32. **Trent Kowalik**, Tony Award-winning actor/dancer/singer (*Billy Elliot*)
33. **Kiril Kulish**, Tony Award-winning actor/dancer/singer (*Billy Elliot*)
34. **Cara-C**, Grammy Award-nominated violinist (vegan)
35. **Kristin Bauer**, actress (*True Blood*) (vegetarian)
36. **Marco Antonio Regil**, popular Mexican TV host (vegan)
37. **Mary Su**, Honorable Mayor Pro-tem of Walnut, California, USA
38. **Marsha McLean**, Honorable Mayor of Santa Clarita, California, USA
39. **Katia Louise**, award-winning filmmaker
40. **Filippa Giordano**, Italian soprano
41. **Elaine Hendrix**, film actress (*The Parent Trap*) (vegetarian)

The inspiration for Supreme Master TV is Supreme Master Ching Hai, world-renowned spiritual leader, humanitarian, bestselling author, poet, and artist. A global pioneer in safeguarding the planet and our future, Supreme Master Ching Hai devotes her time, finances and energy to remind us of our inner goodness and reverence for all of God's creation.

THE PASADENA FOOTHILLS MAGAZINE

Supreme Master Television
Celebrates 5 Year Anniversary

By Justin Kibbe

2011 is Supreme Master Television's five-year anniversary, and to celebrate they're hosting a day-long extravaganza. Festivities begin at 12 noon on Saturday, August 27 at the Pasadena Civic Auditorium, and include a musical, a concert, an art exhibition and a banquet of sumptuous dishes catered by LA's premier vegan restaurants.

Inspired by Supreme Master Ching Hai – a world-renowned spiritual leader, humanitarian, bestselling author, poet, and artist – Supreme Master Television (broadcast from LA) is an international, non-profit channel that focuses on constructive news and programs inspiring peace and outstanding examples of excellence in humanity and noble ways of living. They also advocate for animal welfare, eco-living and vegetarianism. Their channel airs worldwide on 14 satellite platforms, over 90 cable and IPTV networks, as well as live streaming online. To date, they've featured programs in over 60 languages and over 40 language subtitles to serve the global audience.

THE Musical

The Real Love gathers an impressive 40-member cast led by award-winning stars, a 20-piece orchestra, and a team of esteemed composers to present a true love story with all the magic of Broadway. Directed by LA Drama Critics Circle Award winner Chris Shelton, The musical is inspired by a true story about a woman who is deeply in love with her equally tender husband, a doctor. But as their happy marriage blossoms, a calling propels her to make a heartrending decision - remain with her beloved or sacrifice everything in search of happiness for all humanity. In what seems a destined journey, she travels through India and the Himalayas, encountering adventure, danger, and surprises along the way.

THE Concert

The day-long festivities also include a performance by legendary singer/songwriter Don McLean and his band, presenting some of his all-time classic hits – "And I Love You So," American Pie," "Vincent (Starry, Starry Night)," and lots more! Don McLean is one of America's most iconic artists, first hitting the charts in 1971. Over his long and illustrious career, he garnered over 40 gold and platinum records worldwide. In 2004, he was inducted into the Songwriters' Hall of Fame.

THE Art Exhibition

An art exhibition of the creative works of Supreme Master Ching Hai is open to event attendees free-of-charge before and after the show. As a painter, Supreme Master Ching Hai is full of exuberance for nature; as a poet and composer, her romantic heart invokes the deeply human. She is the author of three #1 best-selling books. Her fashion designs deftly weave elegance, comfort, and the flavours of diverse cultures. Her refreshing artistic style is famous for rekindling sparks of joy and tender love inside viewers' hearts.

THE Facts

The grand celebration concludes with a complimentary banquet featuring sumptuous dishes catered by LA's premier vegan restaurants. This one-time event will be recorded and broadcast around the globe on Supreme Master Television. For more information, visit: www. TheRealLoveMusic.com. Tickets are available through Ticketmaster: $35/$45/$55/person: 800.745.3000 or www.ticketmaster.com.